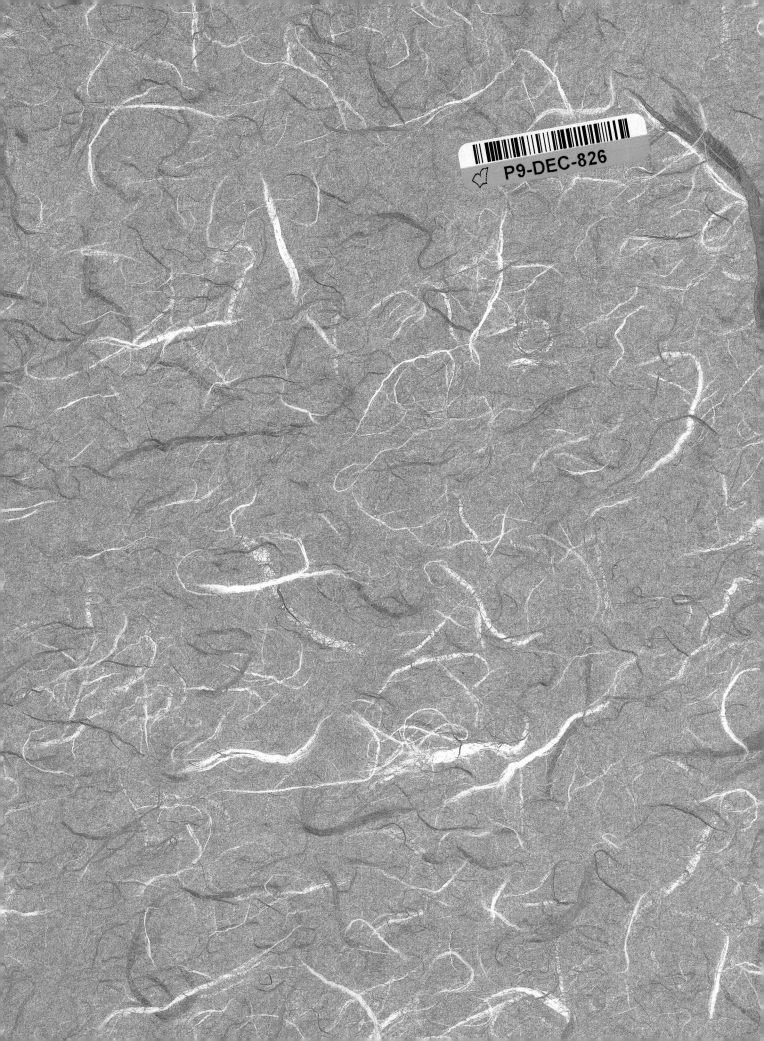

Gourmet LA

Gourmet LA

A Collection of

Fresh and

Elegant Recipes

from the

Junior League

of Los Angeles

Photography by Myron Beck
Design by Lennon & Associates
Published by the
Junior League of Los Angeles, Inc.

Gourmet LA

Copyright 1988
Junior League of Los Angeles, Inc./Publisher

First Edition

Art Direction and Design:
Lennon & Associates, LA
Photography and Set Design:
Myron Beck Studio, LA
Food Styling and Props:
Stephanie Puddy, Pasadena
Lithography:
Hart Graphics, Dallas
Publisher:
Junior League of Los Angeles, Inc.

Library of Congress
Cataloging-in-Publication Data
Junior League of Los Angeles, Inc.
Gourmet LA

88-082365
ISBN 0-9620926-0-6

The Junior League of Los Angeles
is an organization of women
committed to promoting voluntarism and to improving the
community through the effective
action and leadership of trained
volunteers. Its purpose is
exclusively educational and
charitable. The Junior League
of Los Angeles reaches out
to women of all races, religions,
and national origins who
demonstrate an interest in and a
commitment to voluntarism
and to the community.

Cookbook Committee

Chairman	Barbara Van Leeuwen Mullaney 1986 - 1988
	Anne Smith O'Connell 1985 - 1986
Editors	Gayellen Gard Albright*
	Julia Russell Gans*
Editorial Assistant	Cathy Lawless*
Computer	Stephanie Wolfe Ogden
Design	Lucy Hiltabrand Hoover*
Marketing	Barbara Ann Wright
Production	Janet Risi Field*
	Robyn Alisson Watson
Production Assistant	Paula Gaddis Keating
Promotion	Gail Lee
Recipe Collection	Alison Holland Thompson
Recipe Testing	Julia Russell Gans*
Recipe Testing Data Base	Sherry Russell Sclafani*
Secretary	Pamela Shields Diddie*
Treasurer	Joan Tisdall McLaughlin

Committee Members

Marla Robe Alders	Elizabeth Wick James
Kathryn Ackerman Cairns*	Karen Sheahan Johnston
Debora Scalzo Centioli*	Christine Econn Killian
Cynthia Chandler-Hoad	Adrienne John Lang
Dorothy Corcoran	Tanya Lewis
Kathleen Costa	Leslie Henning Lizotte
Andrea Coupe	Mary Sones Martin
Jovon Shaper Courtney*	Maria Mabee Mason*
Leslie Watson Doheny	Margaret Ann Nagle
Christina Hansen Durlacher	Tina Hansen Phillips
Kathleen Mary Everson	Joan Marie Ploetz
Caroline Elizabeth Farwell	Jane Matthews Sample
Mary Ellen Fernhoff	Cheryl Seltzer Shiner
Susan Negrelli Genter	Dian VanDeMark
Sharon Gilliland	Jodi Craig Vettese
Helen Newton Hartung	Cheri Vigna
Sharyn Brickey Hudson*	Ellen Kessler Weitman
Elizabeth Fore Hunsaker	Susan White

* Three year contribution

Introduction

The Junior League of Los Angeles is proud to present a feast of culinary ideas. From the natural bounty that Los Angeles produces and the input of people of many nationalities come food combinations that enhance dining pleasure. Recipes in this collection were contributed by members, friends, chefs, and connoisseurs who have a deep respect for the accomplishments of the kitchen. Ranging from traditional meals to more exotic celebrations, all food concepts reflect Los Angeles' diverse cultures and lifestyles.

Some recipes are simplified and updated versions of old favorites. Others creatively employ less familiar ingredients or methods of presentation. All accent freshness, color, flavor, texture, and fragrance. And each, therefore, is meant to give pleasure to the senses.

There was a deliberate attempt on the part of the committee members to keep the offerings light and elegant. Whether a dish is prepared for a large social gathering or readied for one person, each creation is meant to incorporate quality ingredients and to have a dramatic presentation.

From L.A. to you . . . Enjoy!

Table of Contents

Appetizers

Sunflower Artichoke

1 large artichoke	¼ teaspoon Tabasco sauce
1 quart water	½ teaspoon garlic powder
4 tablespoons cider vinegar	2 tablespoons light cream
1 tablespoon olive oil	¼ teaspoon dried dill
1 bay leaf	¼ pound small cooked bay shrimp
4 black peppercorns	Paprika for garnish
4 ounces cream cheese, softened	Fresh dill for garnish

Slice about ½-inch off top of artichoke to remove main cluster of thorns. Break off small leaves at base. Cut thorny tips from remaining exterior leaves. Cut the stem so there is a flat base. Bring to a boil water, vinegar, oil, bay leaf, and peppercorns. Add artichoke and cover. Simmer for 45 minutes or until leaves loosen and a knife inserts easily into the stem. Remove from pan, drain on paper towel, and allow to cool. Mix together cream cheese, Tabasco sauce, garlic powder, cream, and dill. Pull leaves off artichoke. Spread ½ teaspoon of mixture on tip of each artichoke leaf and top with 2 shrimp. Sprinkle with paprika or dill. Arrange leaves on a round plate or tray in the shape of a sunflower. Clean heart and put in the middle of the arrangement. Spread with cheese mixture and top with shrimp.

Preparation Time: 45 minutes

Cooking Time: 45 minutes

Makes: 30

Note: Shrimp may be marinated in 4 tablespoons oil, 1 teaspoon vinegar, 1 tablespoon water, ¼ teaspoon each: basil, dill, parsley, thyme, and marjoram, 2 cloves garlic, minced, and freshly ground pepper. Marinate for several hours.

Mustard Shrimp in Wonton Shells

12 wonton wrappers
12 medium raw shrimp
Water
¼ pound angel hair pasta
6 tablespoons soy sauce
2 tablespoons rice vinegar
3 tablespoons olive oil
1 small onion, chopped
1 small shallot, chopped

1 clove garlic, minced
1 small green bell pepper, diced
1 small red bell pepper, diced
1 can water chestnuts, thinly sliced
2 tablespoons hot Chinese mustard
½ lime
¼ cup chopped green onions for
   garnish

Preheat oven to 350 degrees.

Oil 12 muffin cups and press in wonton wrappers to form cups. Bake for 12 minutes. Set aside. Boil shrimp for 3 minutes. Peel, devein, dice, and set aside. Boil angel hair pasta for 1 to 2 minutes, drain, and set aside. Combine soy sauce, vinegar, and olive oil in a skillet over medium heat. Add onion, shallot, and garlic. Sauté for 1 minute. Add bell peppers and water chestnuts. Stir for 2 minutes. Add mustard and stir for 1 minute more. Add shrimp to mixture. Stir for 3 minutes and remove from heat. Place mixture in a bowl and squeeze lime over top. Cover and refrigerate for 2 hours, stirring occasionally. Place a small amount of pasta in the bottom of each wonton cup and top with the shrimp mixture. Sprinkle each with green onions and serve.

Preparation Time: 20 minutes
Cooking Time: 10 minutes
Makes: 12

Pumpkin, Crab, and Fennel Purses

Filling

½ carrot

½ stalk celery

½ red bell pepper

½ green bell pepper

½ cup chopped fennel

¼ red onion

¼ teaspoon Tabasco sauce

2 teaspoons minced fresh ginger

1 teaspoon Dijon mustard

2 tablespoons lemon juice

¼ teaspoon nutmeg

2 tablespoons butter

6 ounces crabmeat

¼ cup mashed pumpkin

1 package wonton wrappers

1 egg, beaten

Oil

Chives for garnish

Place carrot, celery, bell peppers, fennel, onion, Tabasco, ginger, mustard, lemon juice, and nutmeg in a food processor. Blend until almost puréed. Sauté mixture in butter for about 6 minutes. Add crabmeat and pumpkin when mixture has cooled. Place 1 teaspoon of filling in center of each wonton wrapper. Brush edges of each wonton wrapper with egg. Gather points of wrapper and pinch to seal. Pleat and gently shape each into a small pouch. Deep fry in oil until golden brown. Tie each with a chive to make a small purse.

Sauce

½ teaspoon minced fresh ginger

½ cup canned apricots

½ cup mashed pumpkin

1 teaspoon Dijon mustard

2 teaspoons port

Purée ingredients in food processor. Serve with purses.

Preparation Time: 45 minutes to 1 hour

Cooking Time: Approximately 30 minutes

Makes: 40 to 50

Pumpkin, Crab, and Fennel Purses; Mustard Shrimp in Wonton Shells.

Spicy Mussels

4 pounds mussels

24 ounces peeled, crushed tomatoes

½ cup chopped cilantro

7 cloves garlic, chopped

1 tablespoon pepper

1 teaspoon paprika

5 basil leaves, chopped

1 onion, chopped

2 cups clam juice

2 cups dry white wine

Clean mussels and place in a steamer. Mix together remaining ingredients. Pour over top of mussels. Steam covered until all mussels open. Serve alone or over pasta.

Preparation Time: 1 hour (includes cleaning the mussels)

Cooking Time: Approximately 5 minutes

Makes: 12 entrees

24 appetizers

Tarragon Marinated Shrimp

2 pounds medium cooked shrimp, shelled, deveined, and tails off

¼ cup safflower oil

¼ cup olive oil

⅔ cup tarragon vinegar

6 tablespoons black peppercorns

2 tablespoons minced fresh parsley

1 tablespoon chopped fresh tarragon leaves

1 white onion, thinly sliced

2 large lemons, thinly sliced

Combine all ingredients in a large bowl. Marinate for at least 3 hours, tossing frequently. Serve with woodpicks.

Preparation Time: 10 minutes

Serves: 6 to 8

Note: Elegant but easy.

Gourmet **LA**

A Perfect Gift!

Please send _____ copies of Gourmet LA @ $24.95 each. If shipped within California, please add 6.5% sales tax. Please include $2.75 shipping & handling per book. Offer good through 12/31/89.

Make check payable to Junior League of Los Angeles or charge to VISA _____ or MasterCard _____ .

Account #   *Exp. date*

Cardholder Signature

Name

Address

City   *State*   *Zip*

Phone (   )

Ship to, if other than above:

Name

Address

City   *State*   *Zip*

Phone orders welcome 213/939-FOOD

Gourmet **LA**

A Perfect Gift!

Please send _____ copies of Gourmet LA @ $24.95 each. If shipped within California, please add 6.5% sales tax. Please include $2.75 shipping & handling per book. Offer good through 12/31/89.

Make check payable to Junior League of Los Angeles or charge to VISA _____ or MasterCard _____ .

Account #   *Exp. date*

Cardholder Signature

Name

Address

City   *State*   *Zip*

Phone (   )

Ship to, if other than above:

Name

Address

City   *State*   *Zip*

Phone orders welcome 213/939-FOOD

Please Send Order To:
Gourmet LA
Junior League of Los Angeles
Farmers Market, Third & Fairfax
Los Angeles, CA 90036

Please Send Order To:
Gourmet LA
Junior League of Los Angeles
Farmers Market, Third & Fairfax
Los Angeles, CA 90036

Tiri Dolmadas

Garlic Yogurt Dip

8 ounces plain yogurt

3 cloves garlic, crushed

¼ teaspoon fresh lemon zest

Combine yogurt, garlic, and lemon zest in a bowl. Make day prior to serving.

Dolmadas

25 to 30 prepared grape leaves

½ cup quick brown rice

½ cup boiling water

5 to 6 tablespoons butter

1 medium onion, chopped

¼ cup fresh lemon juice

½ pound fresh spinach, steamed and chopped

½ cup crumbled feta cheese

Salt

Pepper

Lemon juice

¼ cup warm water or retsina

Rinse and drain individual grape leaves. Set aside. Cook rice in boiling water for about 20 minutes (add more water if necessary). Melt 3 tablespoons butter in skillet. Add onion, rice, and lemon juice. Cook gently until mixture is somewhat dry. Add spinach, feta cheese, salt, and pepper. Mix well.

Preheat oven to 350 degrees.

Lay out grape leaves. Place 1 heaping teaspoon of mixture in center of each leaf. Fold in sides and roll up each leaf. Secure with woodpicks. Place rolled leaves in a baking dish. Dot with butter and sprinkle with lemon juice. Pour ¼ cup water or retsina over leaves. Bake for about 25 minutes.

Pile on a platter and serve with Garlic Yogurt Dip.

Preparation Time: 1 hour

Cooking Time: 25 minutes

Makes: 25 to 30

Tortilla Rolls with Three Salsas

Tortilla Rolls

16 ounces cream cheese, softened
½ cup shredded Cheddar cheese
1 bunch green onions, chopped
4½ ounces chopped black olives
2½ ounces diced green chiles
2 cups cooked diced chicken
   (approximately 4 half breasts)

12 flour tortillas
Cactus Salsa to serve (recipe below)
Salsa Blanca to serve (recipe below)
Salsa California to serve (recipe
   page 19)

Blend cheeses, onions, olives, and chiles together. Stir in chicken until well mixed. Spread about ¹⁄₁₂ of the mixture evenly onto each tortilla. Roll up and place seam side down on dish. Refrigerate for several hours, covered with a damp towel and plastic wrap. Slice into ½-inch slices and bring to room temperature. Serve with salsas.

Preparation Time: 1 hour 30 minutes (includes preparation of salsas)
Makes: 50

Cactus Salsa

1 10-ounce can tomatillos, drained,
   reserving liquid
⅓ cup reserved juice from tomatillos
¼ cup chopped green onions
2 tablespoons chopped fresh cilantro
1 pickled jalapeño pepper

1 tablespoon lime juice
1 teaspoon sugar
½ teaspoon salt
Pinch chili powder
4 ounces prepared cactus strips,
   diced

Purée all ingredients except cactus in food processor. Stir cactus in by hand. Refrigerate overnight or for at least several hours before serving to blend flavors. Serve at room temperature. Makes approximately 2 cups.

Salsa Blanca

⅓ cup Cactus Salsa (recipe above)
½ cup mayonnaise

½ cup sour cream

Blend all ingredients. Refrigerate for several hours to blend flavors. Serve at room temperature. Makes 1⅓ cups.

Continued on next page

Salsa California

1½ ounces stewed tomatoes

8 green onions, chopped

3 cloves garlic, minced

2 tablespoons red wine vinegar

1 tablespoon canned diced jalapeño chiles

1½ teaspoons ground coriander

1 teaspoon cumin

1 teaspoon oregano

¼ teaspoon basil

Salt

Pepper

Crush and chop tomatoes with fork. Blend in remaining ingredients. Refrigerate overnight or allow to stand for at least 1 hour before serving. Serve at room temperature. Makes approximately 2 cups.

Stuffed Potato Bites

1 pound new potatoes (smallest potatoes)

Water

Salt

½ pound bacon

½ cup Very Special House Dressing (recipe page 98)

Fresh parsley for garnish

Fresh dill for garnish

Cook potatoes in boiling salted water until tender. Cut potatoes in half and scoop out insides. Allow to cool to room temperature. Cook bacon until crisp. Drain and set aside to cool. Crumble. Put small amount of crumbled bacon in each potato and top with dollop of Very Special House Dressing. Garnish with parsley or sprig of dill.

Variation

2 tablespoons chopped fresh dill

¼ cup sour cream

¼ cup mayonnaise

1 teaspoon lemon juice

½ teaspoon curry (optional)

Combine dill, sour cream, mayonnaise, lemon juice, and curry. Prepare potatoes as above. Add dollop of mixture to each potato. Garnish with sprig of dill.

Preparation Time: 40 minutes

Cooking Time: 15 to 20 minutes

Serves: 6 (depending on number of potatoes)

Note: Various fillings such as cheese and vegetables may be used. These may be served hot.

Pork Bundles with Peanut Sauce

Pork Bundles

2½ stalks Chinese celery cabbage	1 teaspoon cornstarch
1½ pounds finely ground lean pork	1 tablespoon Chinese rice wine or white wine
2 tablespoons finely chopped green onions	1½ teaspoons sesame seed oil
1½ tablespoons soy sauce	⅓ cup finely chopped bamboo shoots
1 teaspoon minced fresh ginger	1 package small wonton wrappers

Remove cabbage stems and discard. Chop cabbage finely and squeeze out water. Combine cabbage, pork, green onions, soy sauce, ginger, cornstarch, wine, sesame seed oil, and bamboo shoots.

Place 1 tablespoon of filling in center of a wonton wrapper. Gather the points of the wrapper, pleat, and gently squeeze the center. Flatten the bottom and place dumpling on an oiled plate. Repeat process with remaining wonton wrappers. Refrigerate for 3 hours.

Place bundles in a covered steamer and steam for 30 minutes.

Peanut Sauce

4 teaspoons peanut butter	¼ cup soy sauce
1 tablespoon peanut oil	1½ teaspoons minced garlic, about 2 cloves
1 tablespoon sugar	
½ teaspoon cayenne pepper	

Combine ingredients and chill. Warm to room temperature and serve with pork bundles.

Preparation Time: 1 hour to 1 hour 30 minutes

Cooking Time: 30 minutes

Makes: 40 to 50

Note: May be made ahead of time and frozen. Thaw before steaming.

Crisp Chinese Pastries

16 sheets phyllo

1 pound ground pork

8 dried black mushrooms, soaked in hot water

2 tablespoons finely minced fresh ginger

4 green onions, minced

2 eggs

1 tablespoon curry powder

2 tablespoons oyster sauce

4 teaspoons sesame oil

2 tablespoons soy sauce

2 teaspoons sugar

1 cup butter, melted

Hoisin Sauce to serve

Plum Sauce to serve (recipe page 191)

Hot Chinese Mustard to serve

Defrost phyllo according to directions on package. Spread phyllo out and cover with plastic wrap, then a damp tea towel. Always keep phyllo covered.

Brown pork and set aside. Remove tough mushroom stems and discard. Mince mushrooms. Combine pork, mushrooms, ginger, and green onions. Add remaining ingredients except butter. Mix gently but thoroughly.

Preheat oven to 350 degrees.

Remove 1 sheet of phyllo. Cut sheet lengthwise into 2-inch wide strips, working very quickly. Lightly brush each strip with melted butter. Spoon 2 teaspoons of the mixture onto 1 end of each strip. Fold the corner over the filling to form a triangle. Continue folding the strip into the shape of a triangle. Repeat for remaining sheets of phyllo. Place triangles on an oiled baking sheet. Brush tops with melted butter. Bake for 20 minutes. Serve with dipping sauces.

Preparation Time: 20 minutes

Cooking Time: 20 minutes

Makes: Approximately 30

Note: May be refrigerated, covered, for up to 2 days or frozen prior to baking. If frozen, bake for 30 minutes or until golden. Watch for burning.

Poco Calzones

1 pound hot Italian sausage
1 pound mushrooms, chopped
¾ cup minced shallots
3 tablespoons butter
1 tablespoon oil
8 ounces cream cheese, softened

Salt
Pepper
1 package puff pastry, thawed
1 egg
1 tablespoon water
Sesame seeds

Brown sausage, breaking into small pieces. Drain and set aside. Sauté mushrooms and shallots in butter and oil. Stir until liquid evaporates. Allow to cool. Mix in creamed cheese. Add salt and pepper.

Preheat oven to 375 degrees.

Roll pastry to ¼-inch thickness. Cut into 3-inch diameter circles with a cookie cutter or glass. Place a small amount of filling on the pastry. Fold in half and seal with a fork. Beat the egg with water. Brush calzones with the egg and water mixture. Sprinkle with sesame seeds. Bake for 15 minutes or until golden brown.

Preparation Time: 1 hour
Cooking Time: 15 minutes
Makes: 25 to 30

Note: Freezes well after baking.

Mexican Wontons

1½ pounds lean ground beef
1 tablespoon chili powder
½ teaspoon garlic powder
Freshly ground pepper
1 package small wonton wrappers
6 to 8 green onions, finely chopped
2 cups shredded Cheddar cheese

2 cups shredded Monterey jack cheese
Oil
Guacamole to serve (recipe page 40)
Salsa California to serve (recipe page 19)
Salsa Fresca to serve (recipe page 147)

Brown ground beef in a skillet with chili powder, garlic powder, and pepper. Drain. Work with 1 wonton wrapper at a time. Dab edges of wonton wrapper with water. Place 1 tablespoon of meat mixture in center of wonton wrapper. Sprinkle with a small amount of green onion and cheeses. Fold over in the shape of a triangle. Seal edges. Continue in same fashion with remaining mixture. Heat oil in a deep skillet (about 2 to 2½-inches deep). Work with a few wontons at a time. Brown on both sides. Drain on paper towels. Serve with Guacamole and Salsa California or Salsa Fresca.

Preparation Time: 2 hours
Cooking Time: 1 hour
Makes: 40 to 50

Note: Freezes well. To reheat, place frozen wontons on paper towels on a baking sheet in a hot oven at 325 degrees for 15 to 20 minutes.

Swiss Soufflé Puffs

Pastry
8 ounces cream cheese, softened

1¼ cups flour

½ cup butter, softened

Combine cream cheese, flour, and butter in a food processor with metal blade until mixture forms a ball. Refrigerate for 1 hour. Roll out to ¼-inch thickness on a floured board. Cut into 2½-inch circles (approximately 48). Set aside.

Filling
6 ounces shredded Swiss cheese

2 eggs, beaten

½ pint heavy cream

1 tablespoon flour

Preheat oven to 350 degrees.

Blend Swiss cheese, eggs, cream, and flour. Set aside.

Oil mini-muffin cups. Press a circle of pastry into each cup. Bake for 5 minutes. Remove from oven and fill with cheese filling. Bake for 20 minutes or until golden brown and puffy.

Preparation Time: 45 minutes

Cooking Time: 25 minutes

Makes: 48

Note: For variation, add ¼ cup ground walnuts and 1 tablespoon dill to pastry.

Cocktail Biscuits

4¾ cups unbleached flour
3 tablespoons baking powder
1 teaspoon salt
1¾ cups unsalted butter
6 heaping tablespoons solid
    shortening
1½ cups cold milk
3 cups minced mushrooms

6 shallots, minced
Salt
Freshly ground pepper
1¾ cups finely chopped smoked ham
7 green onions, finely chopped
Fresh Herb Cream Cheese (recipe
    page 36)

Combine flour, baking powder, and salt.

Place a third of the flour mixture in a food processor fitted with a metal knife and blend for a few seconds. Add ½ cup chilled butter and 2 tablespoons shortening and process until dough resembles coarse meal. Pour in ½ cup milk and process until blended. Repeat process twice. Wrap dough in plastic wrap and chill overnight or for several hours.

Sauté mushrooms and shallots in ¼ cup butter until tender. Sprinkle with salt and pepper. Add ham and green onions.

Preheat oven to 375 degrees.

Lightly oil baking sheets. Knead dough with mushroom, ham, and green onion mixture. Flour hands and shape dough into 1-inch balls. Place on baking sheets. Firmly indent center of each ball with thumb. Bake for 12 minutes or until golden. Fill centers with Fresh Herb Cream Cheese.

Preparation Time: 45 minutes
Cooking Time: 12 to 15 minutes
Makes: 6 to 7 dozen

Note: Biscuits may be frozen for up to 3 months and warmed just before serving. May fill biscuits with filling of your choice.

Hot Rum Sausages

½ pound pork sausage links
6 tablespoons light rum
2 tablespoons Chinese chile sauce

2½ tablespoons soy sauce
2 tablespoons light molasses
1 lemon, thinly sliced

Cut sausages into 1-inch pieces. Brown and drain. Combine 4 tablespoons rum, chile sauce, soy sauce, and molasses in a saucepan. Add sausage and lemon slices. Cover and simmer for 10 minutes. Heat remaining rum in a separate pan. Pour over sausages and ignite. Spoon mixture into a chafing dish. Keep warm over low heat.

Preparation Time: 30 minutes
Cooking Time: 10 minutes
Serves: 6 to 8

Mandarin Ham Wraps

11 ounces mandarin oranges
1 cup prepared stuffing mix
1 tablespoon chopped chives
8 to 10 slices smoked ham, cut in half
    to make squares

½ cup orange marmalade
1 tablespoon cider vinegar
1 teaspoon Dijon mustard
Parsley for garnish

Preheat oven to 400 degrees.

Drain and reserve syrup from the oranges. Combine the syrup, stuffing mix, and chives. Place 1 tablespoon stuffing mixture and 1 orange segment on each ham slice and wrap from a corner. Secure with woodpicks and place wraps in a shallow baking dish. Combine marmalade, vinegar, mustard, and remaining mandarin oranges, reserving several for garnish. Pour over ham wraps. Bake for 15 minutes. Cut wraps into thirds. Garnish with mandarin orange slices and parsley. Serve with woodpicks.

Preparation Time: 10 minutes
Cooking Time: 15 minutes
Makes: 20

Sage Stuffed Mushrooms

10 ounces bulk sage sausage
1 tablespoon finely chopped green onions
1 tablespoon chopped fresh parsley
¼ teaspoon pepper

1 clove garlic, minced
8 ounces cream cheese, softened, cut into large cubes
40 medium mushrooms
⅓ cup butter, melted

Preheat oven to 350 degrees.

Brown sausage in a medium skillet until it crumbles. Drain. Add onions, parsley, pepper, and garlic. Add cream cheese cubes to the sausage mixture. Remove mushroom stems and discard. Place mushrooms in a shallow baking dish. Brush with melted butter. Stuff mushrooms with sausage mixture. Bake for 20 minutes or until bubbly.

Preparation Time: 20 minutes

Cooking Time: 20 minutes

Makes: 40

Note: This savory sausage and cream cheese mixture offers a delicious new taste in stuffed mushrooms.

Curried Cheese

11 ounces cream cheese, softened
2 teaspoons sour cream
1½ teaspoons curry powder
½ cup real bacon bits
½ cup chopped peanuts

½ cup chopped green onions
½ cup raisins
Chutney
Crackers to serve

Blend cream cheese and sour cream until smooth. Add curry and blend well. Add bacon bits, peanuts, green onions, and raisins. Mix well. Spread into serving dish or form into shape of choice and top with chutney. Serve with crackers.

Preparation Time: 15 minutes

Serves: 6 to 8

Note: All the favorite curry condiments combined in a single appetizing spread. May be topped with peach, mango, or Apricot Chutney (recipe page 189).

Tropical Triangles

2 whole chicken breasts
1 cup unsalted butter
2½ tablespoons flour
1¼ teaspoons curry powder
1 cup milk

½ teaspoon salt
½ cup chopped peanuts
½ cup chopped raisins
½ cup shredded coconut
1 pound phyllo

Preheat oven to 350 degrees.

Bake chicken in oiled aluminum foil for 45 minutes. Remove skin and bone. Cut meat into small pieces. Set aside.

Heat 2 tablespoons butter in a small pan. Add flour and curry powder and cook over low heat for 2 minutes. Add milk and whisk until thick. Season with salt. Stir in peanuts, raisins, coconut, and chicken.

Preheat oven to 400 degrees.

Melt and cool remaining butter. Place 1 sheet phyllo on flat surface and brush with butter. Top with 2 more sheets, buttering each. Cut sheet in half lengthwise, then cut each half crosswise into 6 equal parts. Spoon a teaspoon of filling onto the end of each strip and form a triangle by folding the right-hand corner to the opposite side, as in folding a flag. Continue folding to end of strip. Repeat whole process until all filling is used. Brush triangles with melted butter. Bake on an oiled baking sheet for 10 minutes.

Preparation Time: 1 hour to 1 hour 10 minutes
Cooking Time: 10 minutes
Makes: 50 to 60

Baked Goat Cheese with Garlic and Herbs

½ cup olive oil

4 ounces Montrachet goat cheese (or other goat cheese)

½ tablespoon chopped fresh tarragon

½ tablespoon chopped fresh oregano

½ tablespoon chopped fresh thyme

½ tablespoon chopped fresh basil

½ tablespoon chopped fresh parsley

2 to 3 whole bulbs garlic (approximately 24 to 36 cloves)

½ cup chicken broth

2 tablespoons butter, melted

Sliced French bread to serve

Pour olive oil over goat cheese. Sprinkle tarragon, oregano, thyme, basil, and parsley over cheese and marinate in refrigerator overnight.

Preheat oven to 350 degrees.

Leave garlic intact, but cut about 1-inch from top. Place in ovenproof baking dish. Pour broth and butter over garlic. Bake uncovered for approximately 1 hour. Place container of marinated goat cheese in oven during last 30 minutes of baking until slightly brown and bubbly (do not overbake cheese).

Remove garlic and cheese from oven. Remove skins from garlic. Place garlic and cheese on platter. Spread cooked garlic and cheese on French bread and serve.

Preparation Time: 20 minutes

Cooking Time: 1 hour

Serves: 4 to 6

Note: The whole head of garlic and marinated goat cheese make a very unusual presentation.

Chèvre Pâté with Garlic and Herbs

3 tablespoons hazelnuts
5½ ounces Chèvre cheese (goat cheese), softened
3 ounces cream cheese, softened
2 cloves garlic, minced
5 tablespoons fresh basil leaves
1 tablespoon olive oil

¼ cup grated Romano cheese
1 tablespoon butter, softened
Cheesecloth
Fresh basil for garnish
Ground hazelnuts for garnish
Sesame or water crackers to serve

Chop hazelnuts in a food processor. Set aside. Blend Chèvre cheese, cream cheese, and garlic using pulse method. Set aside. Purée basil, olive oil, and Romano cheese. Add nuts and butter using pulse method.

Line a small, flat-bottomed dish with cheesecloth. Spread half of the creamed cheese mixture in the dish and smooth to the edge. Spread with basil mixture and smooth. Top with remaining creamed cheese mixture and smooth. Cover and refrigerate for several hours or overnight. Invert gently on serving platter and remove cheesecloth. Garnish with basil and ground hazelnuts. Serve with a mild cracker such as sesame or water cracker.

Preparation Time: 30 minutes
Serves: 6 to 8

Pâté with Port and Cognac

½ pound chicken livers
3 tablespoons butter
½ cup chopped onion
8 ounces cream cheese, softened
2 tablespoons minced parsley
½ teaspoon salt
¼ teaspoon pepper
2 cloves garlic, minced

½ teaspoon sage
¼ teaspoon thyme
2 hard boiled eggs
2 tablespoons Cognac
2 tablespoons port
Pumpernickel and rye bread rounds to serve

Sauté livers in butter until light brown. Add onion and sauté. Remove from heat and cool. Place all ingredients except eggs, cognac, and port in a food processor. Blend until smooth. Add eggs, cognac, and port and blend. Refrigerate until serving time. Serve with pumpernickel and rye rounds.

Preparation Time: 15 minutes
Cooking Time: 15 minutes
Makes: Approximately 2½ cups

Chilean Seabass Tartare

Chilean Seabass Tartare is a delicious specialty of the West Beach Cafe.

12 ounces Chilean seabass fillet
1 teaspoon garlic purée
1 teaspoon anchovy purée
¼ cup minced onion
¼ cup finely diced green tomato
1½ tablespoons capers

1 tablespoon chopped parsley
¼ cup Tabasco sauce
Salt
Anchovy fillet for garnish
Sourdough toast to serve

Grind seabass into a bowl. Add garlic, anchovy, onion, tomato, capers, and parsley. Mix well. Stir in Tabasco sauce and salt. Form into oval steaks and garnish with anchovy fillet on top. Serve with sourdough toast points.

Preparation Time: 15 minutes
Serves: 4

Spirited Sausage Pâté

1 tablespoon butter
1 pound hot Italian sausage
1 pound chicken livers
⅔ cup minced onion
¼ cup heavy cream
3 tablespoons bourbon

½ teaspoon salt
½ teaspoon nutmeg
2 cornichons, julienned and fanned for garnish (may substitute gherkins)
Toasted sourdough points to serve

Melt butter in a skillet over medium heat. Remove sausage from casing and crumble into skillet. Brown until cooked through, approximately 5 minutes. Remove sausage with slotted spoon. Set aside. Sauté chicken livers for 5 minutes in sausage drippings. Stir in onion and cook for an additional 2 minutes. Remove livers and onion and blend with sausage in food processor. Add cream, bourbon, salt, and nutmeg. Process until well blended and smooth. Spoon into serving crock. Garnish with cornichons. Serve with toasted sourdough bread points.

Preparation Time: 15 minutes

Cooking Time: 15 minutes

Makes: 2½ cups

Note: Mild Italian sausage may be substituted to make a less spicy pâté.

Pâté Provençale en Croute

Pâté

1 pound chicken livers
4 tablespoons butter
½ cup diced onion
1 cup diced pippin apple or other tart apple
½ cup boursin cheese or Fresh Herb Cream Cheese (recipe page 36)

1 teaspoon nutmeg
2 teaspoons lemon juice
1 teaspoon Worcestershire sauce
2 tablespoons Cognac
½ cup shelled pistachio nuts

Simmer chicken livers with butter for approximately 15 minutes or until fully cooked. Add onion and apple. Remove from stove and allow to cool. Add cheese, nutmeg, lemon juice, Worcestershire sauce, and Cognac. Place in food processor and mix for approximately 1 minute until coarse. Add pistachio nuts and process for 1 minute more. Set aside.

Pastry

8 ounces cream cheese, softened
1 cup unsalted butter, softened
¼ cup sour cream

2½ cups flour
1 egg, beaten

Preheat oven to 375 degrees.

Combine cream cheese and butter. Add sour cream and blend. Add flour and blend. Refrigerate for 1 hour. Roll out dough to a 5×18-inch rectangle about ⅛-inch thick. Spread cooled pâté in center of rolled pastry, leaving a 1-inch boarder around the edge. Fold pastry over pâté. Press along seam and ends to seal. Place seam side down on an oiled baking sheet. Brush with beaten egg. Bake for 25 minutes or until golden brown.

Preparation Time: 40 minutes
Cooking Time: 25 minutes
Makes: 2 to 2½ cups pâté

Nasturtium Spread

Nasturtium literally translated means "twist the nose." This term was coined to describe its peppery punch. Nasturtiums are frequently used for their high vitamin C content.

2 bunches small radishes

1½ tablespoons finely chopped nasturtium leaves, trimmed of stems

2 shallots, minced

1 teaspoon lemon juice

8 ounces cream cheese, softened

Small celery ribs with leaves

1 cucumber, scored with fork tines and sliced to ⅛-inch thickness

Nasturtium flowers for garnish

Grate 1 bunch of the radishes coarsely. Slice the remaining bunch thinly for garnish. Set aside. Blend grated radishes quickly with the nasturtium leaves, shallots, lemon juice, and cream cheese. Fill celery ribs with mixture tucking nasturtium flower in mixture by celery tops. Spread mixture on cucumber slices and garnish with a radish slice standing on edge.

Preparation Time: 30 minutes

Serves: 6 to 8

Note: An additional ½ tablespoon minced nasturtium leaves may be added for extra "bite". The leaves of nasturtiums have a lively peppery flavor similar to watercress. May also be served with crackers.

Nasturtium Spread.

Fresh Herb Cream Cheese

16 ounces cream cheese, softened
3 tablespoons light cream
3 cloves garlic, minced
¼ cup chopped fresh dill
¼ teaspoon freshly ground pepper
1½ teaspoons chopped fresh chives

12 drops Tabasco sauce
¼ teaspoon chervil (optional)
Cheesecloth
Crackers to serve
Sourdough baguettes, sliced

Beat cream cheese. Blend in cream. Add all other ingredients. Line a 1-quart bowl or mold with cheesecloth. Spoon in mixture. Cover and refrigerate for several hours or overnight. Turn out onto a serving board or platter. Remove cheesecloth. Serve with crackers or sliced sourdough baguettes.

Preparation Time: 30 minutes

Serves: 4 to 6

Note: May also be topped with a small jar of black caviar. For serving variation, fill leaves of Belgian endive, split snow peas, or cherry tomato halves with the cheese mixture.

California Artichoke Spread

15 ounces water packed artichoke
hearts, drained and finely
chopped

6½ ounces marinated artichoke
hearts, drained and finely
chopped

2 ounces diced green chiles

2 cloves garlic, pressed

¼ cup shredded Cheddar cheese

¼ cup mayonnaise

¼ cup sour cream

Pepper

¾ cup grated Parmesan cheese,
reserving ¼ cup for topping

Crackers or Garlic Tortilla Crisps to
serve (recipe page 39)

Preheat oven to 350 degrees.

Combine all ingredients except cheese for topping and blend well. Spread into an ovenproof serving dish. Sprinkle top with ¼ cup Parmesan cheese. Bake for 15 to 20 minutes or until golden and bubbly. Serve with crackers or Garlic Tortilla Crisps.

Preparation Time: 15 minutes

Cooking Time: 15 to 20 minutes

Serves: 4 to 6

Wrapped Brie with Blue Cheese

Pastry

2½ cups flour

1 teaspoon salt

1 cup butter

1 large egg

2 tablespoons milk

Blend flour, salt, and butter in a food processor until mixture resembles coarse meal. Add egg and milk while motor is running. Blend until mixture forms a ball. Wrap and chill for 1 hour in refrigerator.

Filling

1 10-ounce Brie wheel

½ cup crumbled blue cheese

¼ cup apricot jam

½ cup sliced almonds

1 egg, beaten

Preheat oven to 350 degrees.

Slice Brie in half lengthwise and sprinkle blue cheese on bottom half, making sure rind is facing down. Place other half back on top. Cover the top with jam and sprinkle with almonds. Roll out pastry. Wrap Brie with pastry, folding ends underneath Brie wheel. Brush pastry with egg. Bake for 30 minutes or until golden.

Preparation Time: 45 minutes

Cooking Time: 30 minutes

Makes: 1 wheel

Note: Frozen puff pastry may be substituted.

Garlic Tortilla Crisps

6 cups oil
1 dozen yellow or white corn tortillas
Salt
Garlic powder

10 to 12 garlic cloves, minced
Salsa Fresca to serve (recipe page 147)
Guacamoie to serve (recipe page 40)

Heat oil in a deep heavy pot or wok. Line 2 baking sheets with paper towels. Cut the stack of tortillas into eighths. Drop 5 to 6 of the triangles into hot oil. Turn them over as soon as they begin to brown lightly, about 10 to 20 seconds. Remove crisps with a slotted spoon to towel lined baking sheets when puffy and golden. Sprinkle salt and garlic powder immediately over crisps. Repeat until all crisps are done. Place crisps in a brown paper bag. Add garlic and shake well to coat crisps. Serve immediately with Salsa Fresca and Guacamole.

Preparation Time: 15 minutes

Cooking Time: 1 hour

Makes: 96

Note: Flour tortillas may be used. May be made a day ahead. Store in a brown paper bag. Recrisp in a warm oven for 5 minutes. Fun to serve with soups and salads.

Guacamole

2 ripe avocados
2 tablespoons fresh lime juice (lemon juice may be substituted)
¼ teaspoon chili powder

2 to 3 tablespoons sour cream
¼ teaspoon salt
⅛ teaspoon pepper
6 dashes Tabasco sauce or more

Halve, peel, pit, and mash avocados. Add remaining ingredients and mix well. Cover with plastic wrap and keep refrigerated until ready to serve (store with 1 avocado pit in the guacamole to keep it from turning brown).

Preparation Time: 10 minutes
Makes: 1¼ cups

Pita Crisps

1 package 6-inch pita bread
½ cup butter
Garlic powder, coarse grind with parsley
Dried oregano leaves

Dried tarragon
Dried dill
1 cup finely grated Romano cheese

Cut around edge of pita bread to make 2 halves. Spread butter on inside of both halves. Sprinkle each half with garlic powder. Separate halves into 3 groups. Top the first group with oregano, the second with tarragon, and the last with dill. Sprinkle each pita with Romano cheese. Broil until golden brown. Cut pitas into fourths. Pitas should be crispy. Fill basket with assorted pita crisps and serve.

Preparation Time: 20 minutes
Cooking Time: 3 to 4 minutes
Makes: 48

Spiced Pecans

2 tablespoons cold water
1 egg white, slightly beaten
½ cup sugar
1½ teaspoons cinnamon

1½ teaspoons ground cloves
1½ teaspoons ground allspice
2 cups whole pecans

Preheat oven to 250 degrees.

Beat water with egg white. Add sugar, cinnamon, cloves, and allspice and beat. Allow to stand for 15 minutes for sugar to dissolve. Toss egg mixture with pecans, coating well. Spread nuts on an oiled baking sheet and bake for 1 hour. Allow to cool in pan. Break up nuts and store in an airtight container.

Preparation Time: 10 minutes

Cooking Time: 1 hour

Makes: 2 cups

Note: May use 1 cup whole walnuts with 1 cup whole pecans for variety.

Rosemary Walnuts

6 tablespoons butter, melted
1 tablespoon dried rosemary
1 teaspoon salt

½ teaspoon cayenne pepper
4 cups whole walnuts

Preheat oven to 325 degrees.

Melt butter and stir in rosemary, salt, and pepper. Toss walnuts with butter mixture to coat. Place walnuts on a baking sheet and bake for 10 to 15 minutes.

Preparation Time: 15 minutes

Cooking Time: 10 to 15 minutes

Makes: 4 cups

Note: Increase cayenne pepper for spicier walnuts. May be made ahead and stored in freezer.

Soups and Stews

Cream of Mulligatawny Soup

2 tablespoons butter
2 onions, diced
2 carrots, diced
2 stalks celery, diced
1 green bell pepper, diced
2 sour apples, peeled, cored, and cubed
4 cups chicken broth
⅓ cup flour

2 cups canned tomatoes plus liquid
¼ teaspoon salt
1 teaspoon pepper
1½ teaspoons curry powder
2 whole cloves
2 sprigs fresh parsley, chopped
¼ cup Madeira, sherry, or white wine
4 cups light cream

Melt butter. Sauté onions, carrots, celery, and bell pepper in a large pot until tender. Add apples and sauté until tender. Add chicken broth. Stir in flour. Add tomatoes, salt, pepper, curry powder, cloves, parsley, and desired wine. Simmer for 2 hours. Add cream and heat through.

Preparation Time: 1 hour

Cooking Time: 2 hours

Serves: 8

Note: Cooked chopped chicken may be added to make a heartier meal.

Avocado Senegalese Soup

1 onion, chopped

1 stalk celery, chopped

2 tablespoons butter

2 tablespoons flour

2 teaspoons curry powder

1 tart green apple, peeled, cored, and chopped

4 cups chicken broth

3 avocados

1 cup light cream

Salt

Shredded coconut, lightly toasted for garnish

Sauté onion and celery in butter until tender. Stir in flour and curry powder and cook, stirring constantly, until thoroughly blended. Add apple and 2 cups broth, stirring to blend. Cook gently over low heat until apples are tender. Transfer to a blender or food processor. Peel, pit, and chop 2 avocados. Add to the apple and broth mixture and blend until smooth. Return mixture to pot. Add remaining broth and cream. Blend well. Add salt and chill. Peel, pit, and slice remaining avocado thinly. Garnish soup with avocado slices and a dusting of coconut before serving.

Preparation Time: 30 minutes

Cooking Time: 30 minutes

Serves: 4 to 6

Country Lentil Soup

5 slices bacon, finely chopped

1 cup chopped onion

1 cup chopped celery

1 cup diced carrots

1 clove garlic, minced

1 cup dried lentils (precooked according to package directions)

1 cup diced potatoes

½ cup tomato paste

2 whole cloves

2 bay leaves

2 cups water

3 cups beef broth

1 tablespoon salt

White pepper

2 tablespoons red wine vinegar

1 cup thinly sliced leeks

2 cups sliced garlic sausage or Polish sausage

Sauté bacon lightly in a large pot. Add onion, celery, carrots, and garlic. Sauté for 5 minutes. Add lentils, potatoes, tomato paste, cloves, bay leaves, water, beef broth, salt, and pepper. Cover tightly and simmer for 2 to 3 hours. Add vinegar, leeks, and sausage just 10 minutes before serving. Simmer covered for 10 minutes.

Preparation Time: 45 minutes

Cooking Time: 2 to 3 hours

Serves: 6 to 8

Pumpkin Tomato Soup

3 tablespoons butter

1 large onion, diced

2 large green onions, chopped

½ cup minced fresh parsley

Salt

Pepper

½ teaspoon dried marjoram

4 cups mashed pumpkin

4 cups chicken broth

1 cup canned crushed tomatoes

1 bay leaf

1 teaspoon summer savory

1 tablespoon lemon juice

½ cup plain yogurt for garnish

Parsley sprigs for garnish

Melt butter in a large pot. Sauté the onions until transparent. Add remaining ingredients. Cover and simmer for 30 minutes. Garnish with a dollop of yogurt and parsley sprigs.

Preparation Time: 30 minutes

Cooking Time: 30 minutes

Serves: 4

Butternut Soup

1 butternut squash, approximately 1 pound
3 tart green apples, peeled, cored, and grated
1 onion, chopped
¼ teaspoon dried rosemary
¼ teaspoon dried marjoram leaves
4 cups chicken broth

2⅔ cups water
2 slices white bread, torn
1 teaspoon salt
¼ teaspoon pepper
¼ cup light cream
Chopped parsley for garnish

Cut squash in half and seed. Combine with apples, onion, rosemary, marjoram, broth, water, bread, salt, and pepper in a large pot. Bring to a boil. Simmer uncovered for 45 minutes. Remove squash from pot. Scoop flesh from squash and discard shell. Return pulp to soup and purée in a blender or food processor until smooth. Return to pot and bring to boil. Reduce heat. Add cream and serve warm with a sprinkle of parsley.

Preparation Time: 30 minutes
Cooking Time: 1 hour
Serves: 6

Spinach Parsnip Soup

4 large parsnips, sliced
2 carrots, sliced
1 large onion, quartered
1 stalk celery, sliced
2 tablespoons chopped celery tops
6 cups chicken broth

½ pound spinach, including stems, washed and torn into pieces
½ teaspoon grated nutmeg
Salt
Pepper

Place parsnips, carrots, onion, celery, celery tops, and broth in a large pot. Cover and bring to a boil. Reduce heat and simmer for 30 minutes. Transfer vegetables with a slotted spoon to a food processor or blender. Add ½ cup of the liquid and purée the mixture until smooth. Add spinach and purée for 30 seconds. Return purée to broth. Add nutmeg, salt, and pepper. Heat gently.

Preparation Time: 30 minutes
Cooking Time: 45 minutes
Serves: 4 to 6

Garlic Bread Soup

6 cloves garlic, sliced
4 tablespoons olive oil
4 slices wheat bread
8 cups chicken broth
½ cup white wine

1 tablespoon paprika
5 eggs, beaten
Garlic Croutons for garnish (recipe below)

Fry garlic slices in olive oil until browned. Add bread and sauté, turning to toast both sides. Add broth and wine. Simmer over medium-high heat until bread is soft. Add paprika and stir, but do not completely break down bread. Pour beaten eggs through a slotted spoon into soup slowly so that eggs rest on top to cook. Serve with Garlic Croutons on top.

Preparation Time: 30 minutes (includes preparation of croutons)
Cooking Time: 2 hours (includes cooking croutons)
Serves: 6 to 8

Garlic Croutons

½ cup butter, melted
2 to 3 cloves garlic, minced
1 tablespoon chopped fresh parsley
Salt

Pepper
4 to 5 cups sourdough or French bread cubes
½ cup grated Parmesan cheese

Preheat oven to 250 degrees.

Melt butter. Add garlic, parsley, salt, and pepper. Drizzle butter over bread cubes, tossing for even distribution. Sprinkle cheese over bread mixture and toss to coat. Spread croutons on a baking sheet and bake for 15 minutes. Toss and bake until crisp and golden.

Preparation Time: 15 minutes
Cooking Time: 15 to 30 minutes
Makes: 4 cups

Note: An assortment of breads such as rye and wheat may be substituted for sourdough or French to add a unique flavor.

Mushroom Velvet Cream Soup

½ pound fresh mushrooms, sliced
1 cup chopped fresh parsley
1 medium onion, chopped
¼ cup butter, melted

1 tablespoon flour
1¾ cups beef broth
1 cup sour cream
Parsley sprigs for garnish

Sauté mushrooms, parsley, and onion in butter, stirring until tender. Stir in flour. Remove from heat and blend in broth. Bring to a boil, stirring constantly. Blend mixture in portions in a blender or food processor with sour cream until smooth. Reheat gently. Garnish with parsley sprigs.

Preparation Time: 30 minutes

Cooking Time: 30 minutes

Serves: 4

Note: A rich and elegant soup enhanced by the fresh parsley.

Asparagus Soup Milanese

4 cups milk
3 cups chicken broth
1 cup cold water
4 tablespoons butter
6 tablespoons flour
2 pounds thin asparagus, tough lower
    ends of spears removed, cut into
    thirds

⅔ cup heavy cream
½ teaspoon salt
½ teaspoon white pepper
¼ teaspoon ground nutmeg
Freshly grated Parmesan cheese to
    serve
Garlic Croutons to serve (recipe page
    48)

Combine milk, broth, and water. Bring mixture to a boil. Set aside. Melt butter in a large pot. Add flour and stir over low heat until cooked and pale (do not allow to burn or scorch). Remove from heat. Beat in hot milk mixture slowly. Add asparagus. Cover and bring to a simmer. Set cover ajar and simmer until asparagus is tender, about 40 minutes. Purée asparagus mixture in a food processor or blender in 2 cup batches. Return to pot. Stir in cream, salt, pepper, and nutmeg. Top with freshly grated Parmesan cheese and Garlic Croutons.

Preparation Time: 20 to 30 minutes

Cooking Time: 40 minutes

Serves: 6 to 8

Cream of Fresh Pea Soup

1 small head Bibb lettuce, quartered and cored

3 green onions, chopped

2 pounds whole peas, shelled (about 2 cups peas)

1 white potato, peeled and diced

3 cups chicken broth

1 cup heavy cream

⅛ teaspoon freshly grated nutmeg

½ teaspoon salt

¼ teaspoon white pepper

2 teaspoons fresh lemon juice

Cross section slices of red bell pepper for garnish

Crumbled bacon for garnish

Chop lettuce with metal blade of a food processor or by hand. Place in a large pot. Add green onions, peas, potato, and 2 cups broth. Simmer covered until potato is tender, about 15 minutes. Remove from heat and allow to cool for 5 minutes. Remove vegetables with a slotted spoon and purée in a food processor or blender. Whisk the purée and remaining ingredients into liquid. Add remaining 1 cup broth. Simmer for 5 minutes. Remove from heat and cool to room temperature. Cover and refrigerate until chilled. Garnish with slice of red bell pepper and crumbled bacon in center.

Preparation Time: 30 minutes

Cooking Time: 30 minutes

Serves: 6

Note: May be served warm.

Cream of Fresh Pea
Soup; White
Gazpacho; Creamy
Carrot Orange
Soup.

Creamy Carrot Orange Soup

4 slices cooked bacon or 2 slices
    Canadian bacon
1½ pounds carrots, sliced
1 onion, chopped
6 tablespoons butter
2½ cups chicken broth
1 cup light cream

¼ cup sherry
1 teaspoon orange zest
Juice from 1 orange
Salt
1 teaspoon white pepper
Pinch freshly grated nutmeg

Crumble cooked bacon or chop Canadian bacon. Set aside. Sauté carrots and onion for 5 to 10 minutes in butter in a large saucepan. Add broth and simmer vegetables until tender. Remove from saucepan and add bacon. Purée mixture in a food processor or blender. Return to saucepan. Add cream, sherry, zest, orange juice, salt, pepper, and nutmeg. Heat gently.

Preparation Time: 15 minutes

Cooking Time: 30 minutes

Serves: 4 to 6

Note: Soup may be frozen before adding cream.

White Gazpacho

3 medium cucumbers, peeled and
    chunked
3 cups chicken broth
2 cloves garlic
2 cups sour cream
3 tablespoons white vinegar
Salt

Pepper
Chopped chives to serve
Chopped green onions to serve
Quartered cherry tomatoes to serve
Smoked almonds to serve
Chopped cilantro to serve

Place cucumbers, broth, garlic, sour cream, vinegar, salt, and pepper in a blender or food processor. Purée until smooth. Chill well. Serve with condiments.

Preparation Time: 15 minutes

Serves: 4 to 6

Autumn Apple Soup

2 tablespoons butter
1 medium onion, chopped
2 teaspoons curry powder
1 tablespoon flour
3 cups chicken broth
1½ pounds cooking apples, peeled, cored, and chopped
1 teaspoon lemon juice

1 tablespoon chopped fresh mint
Salt
¼ teaspoon white pepper
½ cup light cream
4 thin lemon slices for garnish
4 fresh mint sprigs for garnish

Melt butter in a large saucepan. Add onion and sauté over moderate heat for 3 to 4 minutes, stirring occasionally (do not let onion brown). Stir in curry powder and cook for 1 minute, then stir in flour. Pour in broth, gradually, stirring constantly. Bring to a boil. Add apples. Bring back to a boil, cover, and simmer for 15 minutes. Stir in lemon juice and mint. Purée soup in a blender or food processor. Season with salt and pepper. Add cream. Reheat soup gently without boiling. Garnish each serving with a lemon slice and mint sprig.

Preparation Time: 30 minutes

Cooking Time: 30 minutes

Serves: 4

Note: Works well with Granny Smith apples.

Chilled Fresh Cream of Tomato Soup

12 ounces canned peeled tomatoes plus liquid
2 large tomatoes, peeled and chopped
½ onion, chopped
Juice of 1 lemon
1 tablespoon fresh sage or ½ teaspoon dried

1 tablespoon fresh basil or ½ teaspoon dried
Pinch ground nutmeg
½ cup chicken broth
1 cup light cream
Salt
Pepper

Place tomatoes, onion, lemon juice, sage, basil, nutmeg, and broth in a blender or food processor. Blend until almost smooth, leaving some texture. Add cream, salt, and pepper. Mix well. Refrigerate until ready to serve.

Preparation Time: 15 minutes

Serves: 4

Gingered Pear Soup

3 firm ripe pears, peeled, cored, and
   chunked
1 cup water
1 tablespoon sugar
½ teaspoon vanilla or 1 vanilla bean, 6
   to 7-inches long, split lengthwise
½ teaspoon ground cinnamon or 1
   2 to 3-inch stick cinnamon

3 whole cloves
1 slice fresh ginger, cut ⅛-inch thick
   and 1-inch in diameter
3 tablespoons heavy cream
3 tablespoons pear brandy
Mint sprigs for garnish

Combine pears, water, sugar, vanilla bean (or add vanilla later), cinnamon, cloves, and ginger in a saucepan and bring to a boil. Cover and simmer for 30 minutes. Lift pears and ginger from liquid with slotted spoon and place in a blender or food processor. Reserve liquid. Blend pears and ginger until smooth. Set aside.

Bring liquid to a boil in an uncovered saucepan until reduced to about half, about 10 minutes. Remove from heat. Discard vanilla bean, cinnamon stick, if used, and cloves. Stir pear purée into liquid. Add ½ teaspoon vanilla now, if used, cream, and pear brandy. Stir over medium heat for about 5 minutes. Serve hot or refrigerate and serve chilled. Garnish with mint sprigs.

Preparation Time: 15 minutes
Cooking Time: 40 minutes
Serves: 4 first course or dessert servings

Note: This refreshingly spicy soup enhances an autumn dinner on a cold night or cools the palate on a warm summer evening.

Baked Vegetable Chowder

½ pound zucchini, sliced

2 onions, sliced

2 cups garbanzo beans

2 cups chopped canned tomatoes, plus liquid

½ cup butter

1½ cups dry white wine

2 teaspoons minced garlic

1 teaspoon minced fresh basil

1 bay leaf

Salt

Pepper

1½ cups shredded Monterey jack cheese

1 cup freshly grated Parmesan cheese

Preheat oven to 400 degrees.

Combine zucchini, onions, beans, tomatoes, butter, wine, garlic, basil, and bay leaf in a 3-quart baking dish. Cover and bake for 1 hour, stirring at least once after 30 minutes. Season with salt and pepper. Sprinkle with jack cheese and bake for an additional 10 to 15 minutes. Top with Parmesan cheese and broil until cheese is golden.

Preparation Time: 20 minutes

Cooking Time: 1 hour 20 minutes

Serves: 4 to 6

Basque Seafood Chowder

1 onion, chopped

2 large cloves garlic, minced

1 stalk celery, sliced

1 carrot, sliced

¼ cup olive oil

12 ripe tomatoes, puréed and pushed through a sieve, skin and seeds discarded

¼ cup tomato paste

¼ cup dry white wine

1 tablespoon chopped fresh oregano

1 tablespoon chopped fresh basil

1 tablespoon chopped fresh parsley

1 teaspoon chopped fresh thyme

½ teaspoon chopped fresh rosemary

1 bay leaf

3 tablespoons flour, mixed with enough water to make a smooth paste

1 teaspoon salt

½ teaspoon pepper

¼ cup dry Italian olives, pitted and chopped

1 pound fresh fish fillets, cut into large chunks (cod or halibut works well)

½ pound medium cooked shrimp

Sauté onion, garlic, celery, and carrot in olive oil in a large pot until tender. Add tomato purée, tomato paste, wine, herbs, flour paste, salt, and pepper. Simmer for 30 minutes. Add olives, fish, and shrimp. Simmer for another 15 minutes until fish flakes. Stir gently to keep fish in chunks.

Preparation Time: 1 hour

Cooking Time: 45 minutes

Serves: 6

Note: This chowder is best prepared early in the day and refrigerated until evening for flavors to blend. Serve with Zesty Butter Sticks (recipe page 111) or Pita Crisps (recipe page 40).

Hearty Beef, Leek, and Barley Stew

Wine Suggestion:
Zinfandel, Cabernet
Sauvignon, or
Merlot

3 tablespoons butter
1 leek (white part only), chopped
2 stalks celery, chopped
1 onion, chopped
1 pound beef stew meat, cubed
4 cups chicken broth
⅓ cup barley

¼ cup chopped fresh parsley
1 bay leaf
½ teaspoon thyme
Salt
Pepper
1 potato, diced
1 cup light cream

Melt butter in a large pot. Sauté leek, celery, onion, and meat over low heat for about 20 minutes, stirring occasionally. Add broth and barley. Bring to a boil. Add parsley, bay leaf, thyme, salt, and pepper. Cover and simmer for about 2 hours. Add potato. Cover and simmer for about 30 to 40 minutes. Remove bay leaf. Stir in cream. Heat until warm, about 5 minutes.

Preparation Time: 20 minutes
Cooking Time: 2 hours 45 minutes
Serves: 4

Fresh Mussel and Little Neck Clam Stew

Wine Suggestion:
Zinfandel,
Sauvignon Blanc, or
Chardonnay

2½ pounds fresh mussels

2½ pounds fresh little neck clams

1 cup white Spanish sherry

3 cups clam juice

Juice of 1 lemon

¼ teaspoon paprika

1 red bell pepper, seeded and sliced into thin strips

1 yellow bell pepper, seeded and sliced into thin strips

1 green bell pepper, seeded and sliced into thin strips

1 yellow onion, thinly sliced

1 zucchini, sliced 2-inches thick

1 yellow crookneck squash, sliced 2-inches thick

1 tomato, peeled, seeded, and cubed

½ pound smoked Polish sausage, cut into ¼-inch slices

½ cup Greek olives, pitted and quartered

4 tablespoons chopped fresh cilantro

Scrub mussels and clams in cold running water with a stiff brush. Remove the "beard" from the mussel by pulling it sharply. Refrigerate the shellfish while preparing the vegetables. Bring sherry, clam juice, lemon juice, and paprika to a boil in a large pot. Add mussels, clams, vegetables, sausage, and olives. Cover tightly and cook just until all mussels and clams have opened, about 10 minutes. Serve in bowls. Sprinkle chopped cilantro liberally over top.

Preparation Time: 30 minutes

Cooking Time: 10 minutes

Serves: 6 to 8

Fresh Mussel
and Little Neck
Clam Stew.

Turkey Cassoulet

Cassoulet is a
French term for any
dish based on white
beans and various
meats cooked in one
dish.

Wine Suggestion:
Petite Sirah or
Zinfandel

½ pound Great Northern beans
Water
6 pounds turkey, combination of
    drumsticks, wings, and breasts
2 bay leaves
1 carrot, sliced
½ cup chopped celery tops
½ onion, sliced
1 teaspoon black peppercorns
1 teaspoon thyme

1½ to 2 pounds Polish sausage, cut
    into 1-inch pieces
1¼ cups chopped onions
4 cloves garlic, minced
3 tablespoons butter
28 ounces canned plum tomatoes plus
    liquid
2 cups white wine
½ cup chopped fresh parsley
Freshly ground pepper

Place beans in 5 cups of water. Boil for 2 minutes. Remove from heat and allow to stand for 1 hour. Poach turkey in a large pot with enough water to cover, seasoned with 1 bay leaf, carrot, celery tops, sliced onion, and peppercorns, for about 1 hour. Remove turkey. Reserve 6 cups of the turkey broth. Shred meat into long strips. Set aside.

Rinse beans well in a colander. Combine beans with the 6 cups turkey broth, remaining bay leaf, thyme, and sausage. Simmer for 45 minutes. Drain, reserving 3 cups of the broth. Sauté chopped onions and garlic in butter until tender. Stir in tomatoes, wine, parsley, and pepper.

Preheat oven to 350 degrees.

Combine bean mixture, turkey, and tomato mixture with 3 cups reserved broth in a 6-quart casserole or ovenproof pot. Bake covered for 1 hour. Uncover and bake for 1 hour longer.

Preparation Time:　3 hours
Cooking Time:　2 hours
Serves:　6 to 8

Creole Duck Gumbo

*Filé is a powder
made of dried
sassafras leaves first
utilized by the
Choctaw Indians. It
is used to thicken
Creole soups and
stews.*

*Wine Suggestion:
Petite Sirah or
Zinfandel*

**4 to 5 pounds fresh duck, cut into
serving pieces, plus 1 duck
breast, split**

4 tablespoons oil

2 onions, chopped

6 to 8 cups chicken broth

¾ teaspoon thyme

1 bay leaf

1 green bell pepper, coarsely chopped

1 stalk celery, coarsely chopped

1 carrot, coarsely chopped

**½ cup fresh okra, trimmed and cut
into ¼-inch lengths**

**2 fresh tomatoes, peeled, seeded, and
coarsely chopped**

½ cup coarsely chopped red cabbage

¼ cup minced fresh parsley

¼ teaspoon cayenne pepper

Salt

Pepper

4 teaspoons filé powder

Rice to serve

Remove fat and skin from duck and discard. Prick the duck all over with a fork. Brown duck in a large pot over moderately high heat. Remove and set aside. Add 1 tablespoon oil and 1 onion to a large pot and sauté over moderate heat, stirring until golden. Add duck to the pot and add enough chicken broth to just cover the duck. Add thyme and bay leaf. Bring broth to a boil over moderately high heat. Reduce heat and simmer duck for 1 hour 15 minutes or until tender.

Remove duck from broth. Allow broth to cool to room temperature. Remove meat from bones and cut into 2 to 3-inch pieces. Set aside. Strain broth through a fine sieve into a large bowl. Chill for several hours or overnight. Skim and discard fat.

Sauté remaining onion, bell pepper, celery, and carrot in 3 tablespoons oil in the large pot over moderately high heat until tender. Add okra and sauté for 5 minutes. Stir in tomatoes, red cabbage, and 4 cups of the duck broth. Bring to a boil over moderate heat. Reduce heat to a simmer, cover, and stir occasionally for 10 minutes. Add duck meat, parsley, and cayenne pepper. Simmer covered for 5 minutes. Remove from heat. Season with salt and pepper. Add filé powder and blend well. Ladle gumbo into a warmed tureen. Serve over rice.

Preparation Time: 1 hour the day prior to serving, 30 minutes day of serving

Cooking Time: Approximately 2 hours

Serves: 4 to 6

Chili Blanco

1 pound white beans, rinsed
6 cups chicken broth
1 teaspoon chicken stock base
2 onions, chopped
1 tablespoon oil
6 to 8 cloves garlic, minced
7 ounces diced green chiles
4 teaspoons ground cumin
2 teaspoons dried oregano leaves

2 teaspoons cayenne pepper
4 cups cooked and diced chicken
1 cup sour cream
3 cups shredded Monterey jack cheese
Sour cream to serve
Chopped green onions to serve
Chopped cilantro to serve
Chopped tomatoes to serve

Combine beans, broth, and chicken stock base in a large pot. Simmer covered for 2 hours. Sauté onions in oil until golden. Add onions, garlic, green chiles, cumin, oregano, cayenne pepper, and chicken to bean mixture. Simmer for another 30 minutes. Add sour cream and jack cheese. Heat until cheese melts. Serve with sour cream, green onions, cilantro, and chopped tomatoes.

Preparation Time: 30 minutes

Cooking Time: 2 hours 45 minutes

Serves: 4 to 6

Note: May be frozen before adding sour cream and cheese.

Chicken Chili in Flour Tortilla Cups

To make chili powder from dried pods, first roast the chiles on a baking sheet in a 250 degree oven for 8 to 12 minutes. Chiles burn easily, so turn frequently. Allow to cool, then break open and discard seeds. Grind in a coffee grinder.

1 4-pound chicken
Water
2 onions, 1 sliced, 1 chopped
2 cloves garlic, minced
2 bay leaves
1 carrot, sliced
1 celery stalk, chopped
½ cup chopped celery tops
2 tablespoons black peppercorns
2 tablespoons butter
1 green bell pepper, chopped
6 cloves garlic, minced
1 jalapeño pepper, seeded and minced (or 1 canned jalapeño pepper)
12 ounces V-8 juice

28 ounces canned plum tomatoes
15 ounces canned kidney beans, drained
15 ounces canned pinto beans, drained
1 teaspoon ground cumin
¾ cup tomato paste
1 cup reserved chicken broth
2 tablespoons chili powder
4 to 6 flour tortillas
Oil
Shredded Cheddar cheese to serve
Sour cream to serve
Chopped green onions to serve
Guacamole to serve (recipe page 40)

Poach chicken in enough water to cover with the sliced onion, garlic, bay leaves, carrot, celery, celery tops, and peppercorns until tender, about 1 hour. Shred chicken meat and set aside. Reserve broth.

Melt butter in a large pot. Sauté the chopped onion, bell pepper, garlic, and jalapeño pepper until the onion is transparent. Add remaining ingredients except tortillas and oil. Simmer for about 2 hours.

Steam tortillas before frying to prevent tearing. Fry in hot oil in a tortilla basket fryer until golden. Drain on paper towels. Fill with chicken chili. Serve with Cheddar cheese, sour cream, chopped green onions, and Guacamole.

Preparation Time: 1 hour 30 minutes

Cooking Time: 2 hours

Serves: 4 to 6

Note: Best if made a day ahead. Freezes well. Store tortilla cups in a brown paper bag. Another method of making tortilla cups without using the tortilla basket fryer is as follows: Preheat oven to 325 degrees. Rub flour tortillas with oil on both sides. Place tortillas gently down into small Pyrex cups, making soft folds in the sides of the tortilla in order to form a cup. Bake for 15 minutes or until golden and crispy. Allow to cool before removing tortilla cup.

Hot Summer Stew

4 pounds tri-tip beef roast

3 tablespoons flour

½ teaspoon salt

½ teaspoon pepper

½ teaspoon freshly ground nutmeg

2 tablespoons peanut oil

2 bottles dark beer

1 potato, peeled and chunked

2 carrots, sliced ½-inch thick

1 sweet yellow onion, peeled and chunked

1 yam or sweet potato, poached in sugar water until tender and chunked

½ cup peas

1 apple, peeled, cored, poached until tender, and thinly sliced

1 pear, peeled, cored, poached until tender, and thinly sliced

5 bananas, halved and chunked

Preheat oven to 300 degrees.

Cut roast into 2-inch cubes. Coat with flour, salt, pepper, and nutmeg. Brown thoroughly in a skillet with peanut oil. Place meat in an ovenproof pot. Cover meat with dark beer and cook covered for 2 hours. Check occasionally to see that the beer does not cook out, adding more if necessary. Add potato and return to oven for 20 minutes. Add carrots and onion, cooking for another 20 minutes until tender. Add poached sweet potato and peas. Layer top of stew with apple and pear slices and top with bananas. Broil until the fruit topping is heated through, being careful that the bananas do not burn.

Preparation Time: 45 minutes

Cooking Time: Approximately 3 hours

Serves: 6

Southern California Stew

Fresh Salsa

4 medium tomatoes

½ cup coarsely chopped green onions

1 to 2 Anaheim chiles

½ teaspoon ground coriander

Salt

Pepper

Place ingredients in a food processor or blender. Blend until finely chopped. Cover and refrigerate for at least 3 hours for flavors to blend.

Stew

3 pounds beef stew meat, cut into ½-inch cubes

2 onions, chopped

2 cloves garlic, chopped

1 red bell pepper, seeded and chopped

1 to 2 jalapeño peppers, seeded and chopped

2 to 3 Anaheim chiles, seeded and chopped

3 cups beef broth

28 ounces canned tomatoes plus liquid

1 cup corn

2 tablespoons Fresh Salsa (recipe above)

1 tablespoon chili powder

1 teaspoon ground cumin

¼ teaspoon cayenne pepper

Salt

Garlic Tortilla Crisps to serve (recipe page 39)

Shredded Cheddar cheese to serve

Sour cream to serve

Sliced avocado to serve

Fresh Salsa to serve (recipe above)

Brown beef, onions, garlic, bell pepper, jalapeño peppers, and Anaheim chiles in a large ovenproof pot, about 30 minutes. Add broth. Bring to a boil, cover, and simmer for 1 hour. Add tomatoes and simmer for 30 minutes or until meat is tender. Add corn, salsa, chili powder, cumin, cayenne pepper, and salt. Simmer uncovered for 5 to 10 minutes. Line bowls with Garlic Tortilla Crisps. Ladle stew into bowls. Serve with Cheddar cheese, sour cream, avocado, and Fresh Salsa.

Preparation Time: 30 minutes

Cooking Time: 2 hours 10 minutes

Serves: 6 to 8

Salads

Spinach Salad with Warm Smoked Duck and Black Bean Vinaigrette

Fermented black beans are potent, preserved black soybeans, considered to be a major Chinese condiment along with soy sauce and ginger. They are sold in cans or bags in Chinese specialty shops.

Wine Suggestion: Sparkling Rosé or Rosé

Photograph appears opposite Title Page.

Black Bean Vinaigrette

3 ounces fermented black beans	Juice of 1 lemon
Hot water	1¼ cups rice vinegar
½ cup honey	3 tablespoons cider vinegar
⅓ cup Dijon mustard	1 cup oil
1 tablespoon minced ginger	2 tablespoons white wine

Cover black beans with hot water and soak for 30 minutes. Drain well. Set aside. Combine honey, mustard, and ginger in a large bowl. Whisk in lemon juice, rice vinegar, cider vinegar, oil, and white wine until blended. Set aside.

Purée the black beans in a blender a little at a time. Add some of the dressing mixture. Whisk the purée into the remaining dressing. Refrigerate until ready to use. Whisk again before using.

Salad

2 bunches spinach	½ cup sliced shitake mushrooms
2 tablespoons oil	1 package enoki mushrooms for garnish
1 teaspoon sesame oil	2 tablespoons diagonally sliced green onions for garnish
1 cup julienned smoked duck	
¾ cup julienned red bell pepper	
¾ cup julienned yellow bell pepper	

Wash and remove stems from spinach. Drain well and place in a large bowl. Heat oils in a skillet. Add duck, bell peppers, and shitake mushrooms. Sauté for 2 to 3 minutes. Add 1 cup of the vinaigrette to the pan and blend. Pour over spinach, tossing well.

Divide salad among 4 plates and garnish with enoki mushrooms and green onions.

Preparation Time: 30 minutes plus 30 minutes for beans to soak

Serves: 4

Strawberry Chicken Salad

Wine Suggestion:
Chenin Blanc or
Reisling

¼ cup mayonnaise

½ cup sour cream

1 medium shallot, minced

2 tablespoons capers

1 tablespoon caper juice

½ teaspoon salt

¾ teaspoon white pepper

3 tablespoons slivered almonds

4 whole chicken breasts, cooked, skinned, and shredded

1½ cups sliced strawberries

Red leaf lettuce leaves for garnish

Combine mayonnaise, sour cream, shallot, capers, caper juice, salt, pepper, and almonds in a large bowl. Refrigerate for at least 1 hour to blend flavors thoroughly. Toss chicken with sour cream mixture. Add strawberries gently, being careful not to bruise them. Refrigerate for 30 minutes or until thoroughly chilled. Spoon salad onto lettuce lined plates.

Preparation Time: 30 minutes

Cooking Time: 20 to 30 minutes

Serves: 6

Note: Halved avocados, fresh papaya, or pineapple halves may be used as a serving alternative.

Chicken and Bean Sprout Salad

Dressing

¾ cup mayonnaise

2 tablespoons lemon juice

3 tablespoons soy sauce

1½ teaspoons curry powder

1½ teaspoons ground ginger

Combine dressing ingredients. Mix well and chill.

Salad

3 whole chicken breasts, cooked, skinned, and shredded

¼ pound bean sprouts

¾ cup chopped green onions

1 head lettuce (red leaf, curly leaf, or romaine), torn into bite size pieces

½ cup sliced water chestnuts

¾ cup sliced celery

½ cup toasted slivered almonds

Combine salad ingredients in a large bowl. Pour dressing over salad and toss lightly.

Preparation Time: 15 minutes

Cooking Time: 30 to 40 minutes for chicken

Serves: 4 to 6

Note: May substitute ½ pound cooked bay or medium shrimp for chicken.

Elegant Chicken Salad

Curry Powder is not a spice in and of itself, but a mixture of several different spices. A good combination that can be made at home is as follows:

2 teaspoons ground cumin

2 teaspoons ground coriander

2 teaspoons ground tumeric

1 teaspoon ground nutmeg

1 teaspoon salt

½ teaspoon cinnamon

¼ teaspoon cayenne pepper

¼ teaspoon freshly ground black pepper

Mix together and shake well. Store in an airtight container.

Wine Suggestion: Reisling or Chenin Blanc

Dressing
1½ cups mayonnaise
1 teaspoon dried tarragon
¾ teaspoon curry powder
Salt
Pepper

Whisk dressing ingredients together. Set aside and chill.

Salad
4 whole chicken breasts, cooked, skinned, and shredded
Salt
Pepper
2 stalks celery, sliced
¾ cup sliced seedless green grapes
½ cup golden raisins
½ cup diced pitted prunes or purple plums
1 bunch fresh chives, minced
1 cup chopped salted dry roasted macadamia nuts
Red leaf lettuce to serve

Combine salad ingredients and toss with dressing. Serve on a bed of red leaf lettuce.

Preparation Time: 30 minutes

Serves: 4 to 6

Note: Add nuts just before serving if salad is made earlier in the day.

Wine Baked Turkey and Wild Rice Salad

Wine Suggestion:
Reisling or
Sauvignon Blanc

Vinaigrette

¼ cup rice vinegar

4 tablespoons fresh lemon juice

⅔ cup oil

¼ teaspoon salt

1 teaspoon soy sauce

½ teaspoon pepper

2 teaspoons minced fresh ginger

Combine dressing ingredients and chill until ready to use.

Salad

½ breast of turkey

2 tablespoons butter

Water

½ cup white wine

½ cup long grain white rice

1 teaspoon salt

½ cup wild rice

1½ cups tiny peas

4 green onions, minced

¼ cup toasted slivered almonds

½ cup golden raisins

Preheat oven to 350 degrees.

Brown turkey breast in butter in a large ovenproof skillet. Add ¼ cup water and wine and cover tightly. Place in oven for approximately 1 hour 20 minutes or until meat thermometer reads 170 degrees. Remove from oven and allow to cool.

Steam the white rice for 20 minutes in 1 cup hot water and ½ teaspoon salt. Remove from heat. Allow rice to sit for another 15 minutes with lid on. Place in a bowl and fluff with a fork. Simmer the wild rice in 3½ cups hot water and ½ teaspoon salt for 40 minutes or until tender, stirring frequently. Drain the wild rice and add to the white rice. Cook peas for 2 minutes in enough boiling water to cover. Drain. Cut turkey into cubes. Combine turkey with peas, green onions, almonds, raisins, and rice. Toss with vinaigrette.

Preparation Time: 30 minutes

Cooking Time: 1 hour 20 minutes

Serves: 4 to 6

Catalina Shrimp Salad

Wine Suggestion:
Gewürtztraminer or
Sparkling Wine

Dressing

¾ cup mayonnaise

½ cup sour cream

Juice of 1 lemon

¼ teaspoon curry powder

Dash Tabasco sauce

5 to 6 dashes White Wine
    Worcestershire sauce

Whisk dressing ingredients together and chill.

Salad

2 cups small cooked shrimp

1 cup diced celery

½ cup minced green onions

Juice of 1 lemon

1 apple, coarsely chopped

¼ cup chopped green bell pepper

¾ cup chopped fresh pineapple

¾ cup seedless white grapes

2 tablespoons capers

¾ cup slivered almonds, toasted

Combine salad ingredients. Toss salad with dressing and refrigerate until served.

Preparation Time: 30 minutes

Serves: 4 to 6

Note: May substitute crab or chicken for shrimp. May stuff into cantaloupe, avocado, artichoke, pineapple, or papaya halves as a serving option.

Malibu Shrimp and Pasta Salad

Wine Suggestion:
Sauvignon Blanc or
Sparkling Wine

Dressing

⅓ cup sugar

1 teaspoon salt

1 teaspoon dry mustard

⅓ cup white vinegar

¼ small onion, chopped

1 tablespoon celery seed

1 cup oil

Combine dressing ingredients and chill until ready to use.

Salad

1 pound vermicelli

2 pounds medium cooked shrimp

2 cups finely chopped celery

8 ounces finely diced pimento

8 ounces sliced black olives

½ cup chopped fresh parsley

48 green seedless grapes, halved

6 tablespoons mayonnaise

Break vermicelli into 2-inch pieces and cook according to package directions. Drain and rinse under cold water. Combine with shrimp, celery, pimento, olives, parsley, and grapes. Toss with 1 cup of dressing. Add mayonnaise and mix. Marinate overnight. Reserve extra dressing and add to salad just before serving, if needed.

Preparation Time: 30 minutes

Cooking Time: 10 minutes

Serves: 8 to 10

Warm Crab Papaya Salad

Wine Suggestion:
Reisling or
Chenin Blanc

½ bunch watercress
1 large head Bibb lettuce, chopped
1 papaya, cubed
1 tomato, cubed
2 tablespoons butter
1½ pounds crab meat, legs if
    available

Pepper
⅓ cup oil
3 tablespoons red wine vinegar
2 ounces brandy
Salt

Chop half of the watercress, reserving half for garnish. Combine chopped watercress, lettuce, papaya, and tomato. Set aside. Melt butter in a skillet. Add crab and season with pepper. Sauté slowly, until warm, turning frequently. Remove crab from skillet. Reserve juices. Raise heat and add oil, vinegar, and brandy. Season with salt and pepper. Add crab to salad and toss with dressing. Garnish with remaining watercress.

Preparation Time: 30 minutes
Cooking Time: 10 to 15 minutes
Serves: 4

Cold Roast Beef Salad with Crumbled Blue Cheese

Wine Suggestion:
Pinot Gris or
Sparkling Rosé

Dressing

½ cup olive oil

¼ cup red wine vinegar

2 teaspoons Dijon mustard

½ teaspoon sugar

Salt

¼ teaspoon pepper

1 clove garlic, crushed

2 tablespoons finely chopped fresh parsley

Blend dressing ingredients and chill until ready to use.

Salad

1½ pounds cold rare "Deli" roast beef, sliced to medium thickness and julienned

12 mushrooms, sliced

12 cherry tomatoes, halved

1 red onion, thinly sliced

1 avocado, cubed

3 tablespoons crumbled blue cheese

Combine all salad ingredients except the avocado and blue cheese. Toss salad with dressing. Add avocado and toss gently. Sprinkle with blue cheese.

Preparation Time: 15 minutes

Serves: 6 to 8

Note: Dressing may be made ahead. Salad is best if made just before serving.

Chilled Steak Salad

Wine Suggestion:
Pinot Gris, Sparkling
Wine, or Rosé

2 pounds boneless top sirloin, salted, peppered, and cooked to medium rare
2 tablespoons red wine vinegar
1 egg
1 tablespoon Dijon mustard
½ cup oil
1 tablespoon minced fresh chives
1 tablespoon minced fresh dill

16 ounces hearts of palm, sliced
1 bunch green onions, chopped
½ pound mushrooms, sliced
½ pound snow peas
10 cherry tomatoes, halved
½ teaspoon salt
½ teaspoon pepper

Slice steak very thin. Set aside.

Blend vinegar, egg, mustard, oil, chives, and dill in a food processor or blender until smooth. Set aside.

Combine steak, vegetables, salt, and pepper in large bowl. Pour dressing over salad and toss. Allow to stand for about 1 hour before serving. Best if made the day served.

Preparation Time: 30 minutes

Cooking Time: 15 to 20 minutes for steak

Serves: 6

Note: This salad has a wonderful medley of flavors and textures.

Marinated Picnic Carrots

2 pounds carrots, sliced on the
    diagonal
⅔ cup cider vinegar
½ cup oil
½ cup sugar

½ cup chopped onion
1 package Italian seasoned salad
    dressing mix
¼ cup chopped parsley

Boil or steam carrots until tender but crisp. Cool. Blend all other ingredients except parsley. Pour over cooled carrots and toss. Marinate for several hours or overnight in refrigerator. Add parsley just before serving and toss.

Preparation Time: 15 minutes

Cooking Time: 15 minutes

Serves: 6 to 8

Note: Best if marinated overnight. This colorful salad goes well with a summer picnic or barbeque.

Asparagus with Sesame Oil Vinaigrette

2 pounds asparagus
1 teaspoon minced garlic
½ teaspoon salt
½ teaspoon white pepper
2 teaspoons Dijon mustard

1½ teaspoons fresh lemon juice
4 tablespoons sesame oil
1 tablespoon toasted sesame seeds
    for garnish

Cut off tough lower ends of asparagus spears and discard. Steam asparagus until tender. Drain and run under cold water. Dry thoroughly. Set aside. Blend remaining ingredients in a blender. Pour over asparagus. Sprinkle with toasted sesame seeds.

Preparation Time: 15 minutes

Cooking Time: Approximately 15 minutes for asparagus

Serves: 4 to 6

English Cucumber Salad

2 red onions, cut into ¼-inch thick slices

3 English cucumbers, cut into ½-inch thick slices

6 ounces whole black medium pitted olives

6 vine-ripened tomatoes, cut in wedges

4 tablespoons chopped fresh dill

2 cups raspberry vinegar

Feta cheese for garnish

Cut onion rings in half. Combine onions, cucumbers, olives, tomatoes, and dill. Pour vinegar over ingredients and toss. Allow to marinate for a minimum of 4 hours. Sprinkle with crumbled feta cheese.

Preparation Time: 30 minutes

Serves: 6

Leek Salad with Vinaigrette Dressing

3 leeks, sliced lengthwise (white part plus ½-inch of green)

½ cup white wine vinegar

½ cup olive oil

15 black peppercorns

2 bay leaves

½ cup sliced celery

4 tablespoons chopped fresh parsley

Salt

Water

Place leeks in a skillet. Combine vinegar and oil and pour over leeks. Add remaining ingredients and enough water to cover. Simmer covered for 20 minutes. Simmer uncovered to reduce liquid, if desired. Remove bay leaves and serve warm.

Preparation Time: 15 minutes

Cooking Time: 20 minutes

Serves: 4 to 6

Celery Hearts and Bell Peppers in Vinaigrette

Vinaigrette

⅔ cup olive oil

⅓ cup white wine vinegar

½ teaspoon fresh lemon juice

1 clove garlic, pressed or minced

Salt

Pepper

Combine all ingredients and mix well. Chill until ready to use.

Salad

2 pounds large celery hearts

Water

½ medium yellow bell pepper, sliced into strips

½ medium red bell pepper, sliced into strips

¼ cup crumbled blue cheese

Cut celery hearts lengthwise into quarters. Wash well. Cut quarters into 6 to 8-inch lengths. Bring 1-inch of water to a boil in a large skillet. Add celery hearts and simmer covered until just tender, about 10 to 12 minutes. Remove from skillet and plunge into ice water to stop the cooking process. Drain well. Place on a serving dish. Pour vinaigrette over celery hearts, cover, and chill for at least 1 hour or up to 24 hours, turning celery hearts occasionally. Arrange strips of bell peppers over celery hearts. Sprinkle with blue cheese and serve.

Preparation Time: 30 minutes

Cooking Time: 10 to 12 minutes

Serves: 8

Note: A very elegant and dramatic salad.

Watercress Salad with Walnut Vinaigrette

Watercress is a perennial cress of the mustard family. It is a water loving plant with a mildly pungent flavor used in salads or as a seasoning.

2 tablespoons white wine vinegar
1 teaspoon Dijon mustard
1 small shallot, minced
Salt
Freshly ground pepper
Pinch sugar

5 tablespoons walnut oil
1 teaspoon chopped chives
4 bunches watercress
½ cup walnuts
¼ cup shredded Gruyère cheese

Whisk vinegar, mustard, shallot, salt, pepper, and sugar together. Pour in walnut oil slowly while whisking. Add chives. Chop watercress coarsely and sprinkle with walnuts. Add ½ to ¾ of dressing in spoonfuls, then top with Gruyère cheese.

Preparation Time: 15 minutes

Serves: 4

Note: Salad does not keep after mixed. Dressing will keep for 2 to 4 days in refrigerator. May substitute Danish blue cheese for Gruyère cheese.

Tossed Salad with Beets Tarragon

16 ounces pickled beet slices, drained
1 red onion, thinly sliced into rings
1 head curly leaf lettuce or 2 heads
    Bibb lettuce, torn into small
    pieces
¼ cup sour cream
¼ cup mayonnaise

2 teaspoons tarragon vinegar
¼ teaspoon thyme
1 teaspoon salt
¼ teaspoon pepper
Lettuce leaves to serve

Drain beets on paper towels to remove excess moisture. Cut beets into julienne strips and chill. Toss beets, onion, and lettuce together. Reserve a few beets and onion rings for garnish.

Combine sour cream, mayonnaise, vinegar, thyme, salt, and pepper. Toss with salad mixture. Serve on lettuce lined salad plates. Garnish with reserved beets and onion rings.

Preparation Time: 15 minutes

Serves: 6

Field Salad with Champagne Dressing

Other edible flowers are carnation, chrysanthemum, Bachelor's button, dandelion, hibiscus, hollyhock, magnolia, primrose, rose, and violet. Caution: Many flowers are non-edible and poisonous. Check before using.

Champagne Dressing

4 tablespoons champagne vinegar
4 whole shallots, chopped
2 cloves garlic, minced
⅔ cup light olive oil

½ cup fresh basil
4 medium nasturtium leaves
Salt
Pepper

Combine all ingredients in a blender or food processor. Blend well and refrigerate until ready to use.

Salad

2 bunches watercress, leaves only
2 small heads Bibb lettuce, leaves separated
3 small heads radicchio
4 heads Belgian endive

3 tablespoons coarsely chopped fresh basil
24 flowers (nasturtiums, pansies, marigolds, petunias, or thyme flowers), at least 3 per plate for garnish

Wash all greens and pat dry. Tear greens into small pieces. Add basil and toss. Place greens onto serving plates. Garnish with at least 3 flowers per plate. Drizzle with dressing.

Preparation Time: 30 minutes

Serves: 6 to 8

Note: The dressing for this salad has the consistency and color of a pesto sauce. The nasturtium leaves give it a peppery flavor. Nasturtium flowers have a soft velvety texture which lend a wonderful contrast to the greens. May add or substitute romaine, arugula, mache, or curly leaf lettuce.

Field Salad with Champagne Dressing.

Spicy Thai Coleslaw

1 cup dry roasted peanuts
2 cloves garlic
2 serrano chiles, stems, tips, and
    seeds removed
1 pound green cabbage, cored and
    cut into wedges
½ pound cucumbers, peeled, seeded,
    and quartered lengthwise

4 green onions
¼ cup rice vinegar
2 tablespoons sugar
½ teaspoon curry powder
½ cup oil
1 tablespoon chopped fresh cilantro
1 tablespoon chopped fresh parsley

Chop peanuts with metal blade in a food processor with 6 to 8 pulses. Place in a large bowl. Drop garlic and chiles through feed tube of processor with motor running, until chopped. Add to peanuts. Slice cabbage across the grain with the slicing blade. Add to peanuts and chiles. Slice cucumbers. Chop green onions by hand. Add cucumbers and onions to cabbage and toss. Whisk vinegar, sugar, curry, and oil together. Pour over coleslaw. Add cilantro and parsley and toss.

Preparation Time: 30 minutes

Serves: 6 to 8

Note: This is a hot and spicy salad with a lot of zing. Reduce amount of chile for less spice.

Spinach Salad with Curry Dressing

Curry Dressing

⅔ cup oil

½ cup vinegar (cider, white wine, or
    raspberry)

1 tablespoon finely chopped chutney

1 teaspoon curry powder

1 teaspoon dry mustard

1 teaspoon salt

½ teaspoon white pepper

¼ teaspoon Tabasco sauce

Combine ingredients using the metal blade of a food processor. Allow to stand at room temperature for 2 hours so that the flavors will blend.

Salad

2 bunches fresh spinach, washed and
    torn into small pieces

3 Red Delicious apples, cored and
    thinly sliced

1 cup golden raisins

⅔ cup cashews

2 to 4 green onions, thinly sliced

2 tablespoons sesame seeds, toasted

½ pound bacon, cut into squares and
    cooked until crisp

Combine salad ingredients in a large bowl. Toss salad with dressing just before serving.

Preparation Time: 45 minutes

Serves: 6 to 8

Fresh Spinach and Basil Salad

Proscuitto is a salted ham which is cured by drying and is always sliced paper thin.

6 cups fresh spinach leaves, rinsed and dried

2 cups fresh basil leaves, rinsed and dried

½ cup olive oil

3 cloves garlic, finely chopped

½ cup pine nuts

4 ounces prosciutto, diced

Salt

Pepper

¾ cup freshly grated Parmesan cheese

Toss spinach and basil together in a large bowl. Heat oil in a skillet over medium heat. Add garlic and pine nuts. Sauté until the nuts begin to brown slightly. Stir in proscuitto and sauté for 1 minute. Season with salt and pepper. Toss spinach and basil with warm dressing and sprinkle with Parmesan cheese. Serve immediately.

Preparation Time: 30 minutes

Cooking Time: 5 minutes

Serves: 4 to 6

Note: May substitute ham for proscuitto.

Tomato, Basil, and Pasta Salad

12 ounces tricolor spiral pasta

½ cup extra virgin olive oil

4 tablespoons fresh lemon juice

3 tablespoons red wine vinegar

2 cloves garlic, minced

Freshly ground black pepper

¼ cup chopped green bell pepper

¼ cup chopped pimentos

¼ cup grated carrots

¼ cup chopped spinach

½ cup cubed provolone cheese

3½ cups diced Italian plum tomatoes

1 cup chopped and firmly packed fresh basil

Cook pasta according to package directions. Drain. Whisk olive oil, lemon juice, vinegar, garlic, and pepper together. Add to pasta and toss. Refrigerate until cool. Add bell pepper, pimentos, carrots, spinach, and cheese. Toss in tomatoes and basil just before serving.

Preparation Time: 30 minutes

Serves: 8 to 10

Tortellini Salad

Dressing

½ cup finely chopped parsley

2 cloves garlic, minced

¼ cup olive oil

2 tablespoons grated Parmesan cheese

1 tablespoon red wine vinegar

Whisk dressing ingredients together shortly before serving.

Salad

1 pound cheese filled tortellini

¼ cup olive oil

½ pound prosciutto, sliced ¼-inch and cubed

½ pound smoked turkey, sliced ¼-inch and cubed

½ pound provolone cheese, cubed

1 cup peas

2 carrots, grated

½ large red bell pepper, thinly sliced

Cook tortellini according to package directions, about 8 to 10 minutes. Place in a large bowl and toss with olive oil. Add prosciutto, turkey, provolone cheese, peas, carrots, and bell pepper and toss. Cover and refrigerate for 30 minutes. Pour dressing over salad and toss.

Preparation Time: 45 minutes

Cooking Time: 8 to 10 minutes for tortellini

Serves: 6

Note: May substitute ham for prosciutto. A hearty, colorful main dish salad.

Minted Wild Rice Salad

Wild rice is not a true rice, but the seed of a wild water grass native to the North American Great Lake states. The grass yields a long, slender grain with a distinctive sweet, nutty flavor.

1 cup wild rice, uncooked
1 green bell pepper, chopped
6 to 8 green onions, chopped
½ cup chopped fresh mint
⅔ cup raisins
⅔ cup coarsely chopped pecans

2 tomatoes, chopped
½ cup fresh lemon juice
½ cup olive oil
½ teaspoon freshly ground pepper
¼ teaspoon salt

Cook wild rice according to package directions. Drain and cool. Add bell pepper, onions, mint, raisins, pecans, and tomatoes. Set aside. Mix together lemon juice, oil, salt, and pepper. Combine with wild rice mixture. Marinate in refrigerator for several hours or overnight.

Preparation Time: 45 minutes

Cooking Time: 30 minutes

Serves: 6 to 8

Note: May be stored in refrigerator for up to 5 days.

Panzanella Bread Salad

4 whole crusty scissor rolls, cut into bite sized cubes
1 beefsteak tomato, cubed
⅓ cup chopped red onion
1½ large cucumbers, peeled and chunked
⅓ cup chopped red or yellow bell pepper

1 tablespoon capers, drained
⅓ cup chopped white onion
⅔ cup olive oil
⅓ cup red wine vinegar
2 tablespoons crumbled feta cheese

Layer bread, tomato, red onion, cucumbers, bell pepper, capers, and white onion in a large glass bowl. Whisk oil and vinegar together. Pour over salad just before serving. Sprinkle with feta cheese. Serve tossed or layered depending on personal preference.

Preparation Time: 30 minutes

Serves: 4

Note: May substitute sourdough or French bread for scissor rolls.

Molded Gazpacho Salad with Avocado Dressing

Avocado Dressing

1 avocado	1 teaspoon salt
½ cup sour cream	⅛ teaspoon sugar
½ cup light cream	1 clove garlic, crushed
1 tablespoon grated onion	1 tablespoon fresh lemon juice

Peel avocado and remove pit. Place in a food processor or blender. Add all ingredients and blend until smooth. Cover and refrigerate until ready to serve.

Salad

2 envelopes unflavored gelatin	2 tomatoes, peeled and diced
2¼ cups tomato juice or Snappy Tom	1 cucumber, peeled and diced
⅓ cup red wine vinegar	¼ cup finely chopped red onion
1 teaspoon salt	1 tablespoon chopped fresh chives
1 teaspoon Tabasco sauce (optional if using Snappy Tom)	Parsley or cilantro sprigs for garnish

Sprinkle gelatin over ¾ cup tomato juice in a medium saucepan. Cook over low heat, stirring constantly until gelatin is dissolved. Remove from heat. Stir in remaining juice, vinegar, salt, and Tabasco sauce (if using tomato juice). Place mixture in freezer, stirring occasionally until it has the consistency of unbeaten egg whites, about 30 to 45 minutes. Fold in remaining ingredients when mixture is thick and pour into a 1½-quart flat mold (ring or otherwise) that has been oiled. Refrigerate for 6 hours until firm. Unmold salad by running a small spatula around the edges. Invert over a serving platter and place a hot damp dish towel over the inverted mold and shake gently to release. Garnish with parsley or cilantro. Serve with Avocado Dressing.

Preparation Time: 1 hour

Serves: 6 to 8

Note: May be made up to 5 days ahead. May substitute sour cream for Avocado Dressing if avocados are not in season.

Frozen Raspberry Salad with Blueberries

1 small package raspberry flavored
    gelatin
1 cup hot water
1 package frozen raspberries, partially
    thawed
6 ounces cream cheese, softened
1 cup sour cream

16 ounces jellied cranberry sauce
Salt
Fresh mint leaves for garnish
Fresh raspberries for garnish
Fresh blueberries for garnish
Whipped cream for garnish

Dissolve gelatin in hot water. Add raspberries and stir until berries separate. Set aside. Blend cream cheese, sour cream, and cranberry sauce in a blender or food processor until smooth. Stir in gelatin mixture gently. Add salt and blend. Pour into a shallow mold if chilling in refrigerator or into a deep ring mold if freezing. Chill or freeze until firm. Garnish with mint leaves, raspberries, blueberries, and whipped cream (do not serve on lettuce leaves).

Preparation Time: 30 minutes plus several hours chilling time
Serves: 8 to 10

Fruited Green Salad with Ginger Orange Dressing

Ginger Orange Dressing

½ cup oil

2 tablespoons honey

¼ teaspoon ground ginger

4 tablespoons thawed orange juice concentrate

½ teaspoon salt

Whisk dressing ingredients together. Chill until ready to use.

Salad

2 large or 3 small heads Bibb or butter lettuce

1 cup chunked pineapple

1 large ripe peach, peeled and sliced

½ cup halved red seedless grapes

1 cup cubed Swiss cheese

½ cup walnut halves

Rinse and dry lettuce leaves. Tear lettuce into bite size pieces in a large bowl. Add remaining ingredients just before serving and toss with Ginger Orange Dressing.

Preparation Time: 30 minutes

Serves: 6

Note: The combination of fresh summer fruits and greens tossed with the Ginger Orange Dressing provides an ideal salad for warm weather entertaining. Canned pineapple tidbits or chunks may be substituted if fresh pineapple is unavailable.

Papaya and Avocado Salad with Papaya Seed Dressing

2 papayas, peeled, seeded, cubed, and seeds reserved
1 cup oil
½ cup tarragon vinegar
¼ cup sugar
2 tablespoons lime juice
2 teaspoons salt

1 teaspoon dry mustard
2 tablespoons chopped onion
½ teaspoon paprika
2 avocados, peeled, pitted, and cubed
Red or green leaf lettuce leaves to serve

Combine 1½ to 2 tablespoons of the reserved papaya seeds, oil, vinegar, sugar, lime juice, salt, dry mustard, onion, and paprika in blender or food processor. Blend until seeds look like ground pepper. Lay papaya and avocado on lettuce lined plates. Top with dressing.

Preparation Time: 20 minutes
Serves: 4

Note: Dressing may be served over cooked cubed chicken, fresh fruit, and/or greens.

Farmers Market Fruit Salad with Lime Dressing

Farmers Market has been the home of the Junior League of Los Angeles for the past 16 years.

Lime Dressing

½ cup oil

2 tablespoons honey

5 tablespoons thawed limeade concentrate

½ small green apple, chopped

Whisk dressing ingredients together. Chill until ready to use.

Salad

1 large nectarine, cubed

1 large red plum, cubed

1 large black plum, cubed

2 large star fruits, sliced widthwise (optional)

1 large green apple, cubed

1 red d'Anjou pear, cubed

1½ cups fresh pineapple, cubed

1 cup halved seedless red grapes

1 cup halved seedless green grapes

1 large banana, sliced

1 cup fresh blueberries

1 cup halved fresh strawberries

1 large kiwi, peeled and sliced

½ papaya, peeled, seeded, and cubed

Combine fruit in a large bowl. Pour dressing over fruit and toss gently (if mixing fruit ahead, squeeze fresh lemon juice over top and toss gently). Cover and refrigerate until ready to serve.

Preparation Time: 30 minutes

Serves: 6 to 8

Note: The lime dressing enhances the unique flavors of the many fruits. Any combination of fruits works well with this dressing.

Strawberry and Grapefruit Salad with Strawberry Vinaigrette

Strawberry Vinaigrette

8 strawberries	⅓ cup honey
1 cup oil	1 teaspoon dry mustard
½ cup white vinegar	1 teaspoon celery seed
¼ cup pink grapefruit juice	1 teaspoon paprika

Mix all dressing ingredients in a blender. Chill until ready to use.

Salad

3 heads Bibb lettuce	24 strawberries, halved
3 pink grapefruit, peeled, quartered, and sliced	

Break apart 1 head of lettuce into separate leaves. Arrange lettuce leaves on individual salad plates. Tear remaining 2 heads of lettuce into small pieces. Divide torn lettuce onto salad plates. Place grapefruit slices on top of the lettuce. Top with 6 strawberry halves in the center of each salad. Drizzle with Strawberry Vinaigrette.

Preparation Time: 30 minutes

Serves: 6 to 8

Strawberry and
Grapefruit Salad
with Strawberry
Vinaigrette.

French Potato Salad

8 medium potatoes, peeled and boiled until tender
½ cup diced celery
½ cup sliced water chestnuts, drained
¼ cup slivered almonds, toasted
¼ cup chopped red onion
½ cup chopped green onions
2 hard-boiled eggs, sliced
¼ cup chopped red bell pepper

2 tablespoons minced fresh parsley
2 teaspoons salt
¼ teaspoon pepper
½ teaspoon celery seed
2 cups sour cream
4 ounces crumbled blue cheese
¼ cup white wine vinegar
Lettuce leaves to serve

Cube potatoes. Add celery, water chestnuts, almonds, onions, eggs, bell pepper, parsley, salt, pepper, and celery seed and toss. Combine sour cream, blue cheese, and vinegar and mix well. Pour over potato mixture and toss lightly. Chill overnight. Serve on lettuce leaves.

Preparation Time: 30 minutes
Cooking Time: Approximately 20 minutes for potatoes
Serves: 6 to 7

Raspberry Vinaigrette

½ clove garlic
½ teaspoon sugar
1½ teaspoons lemon juice
½ teaspoon salt
½ teaspoon pepper
¾ teaspoon dry mustard

1 cup light olive oil
¼ cup water
¼ cup plus 2 tablespoons raspberry vinegar
½ teaspoon White Wine Worcestershire sauce

Mince garlic by dropping through feed tube of food processor with motor running. Add sugar, lemon juice, salt, pepper, and dry mustard. Blend for 10 seconds until ingredients are well mixed. Add oil very slowly with motor running. Add water, raspberry vinegar, and White Wine Worcestershire sauce. Pour into a covered container and chill until ready to use.

Preparation Time: 15 minutes
Makes: 1½ cups

Creamy Gorgonzola Dressing

1 egg
2 tablespoons red wine vinegar
2 tablespoons cream
1 tablespoon lemon juice
Pinch sugar
½ teaspoon Dijon mustard

2 cloves garlic, crushed
½ cup oil
3 tablespoons olive oil
¼ pound Gorgonzola cheese, crumbled

Blend egg, vinegar, cream, lemon juice, sugar, mustard, and garlic in a blender or food processor. Add oil slowly with motor running (the mixture will not be thick). Add half of the Gorgonzola cheese and blend. Fold in remaining crumbled cheese. Refrigerate until ready to use.

Preparation Time: 5 minutes

Makes: Approximately 1½ cups

Note: Dressing will keep up to 5 or 6 days in refrigerator.

Dill Dijon Dressing

½ cup mayonnaise
1 tablespoon tarragon vinegar
1 tablespoon Dijon mustard

1 tablespoon olive oil
Pepper
1 teaspoon dill

Combine ingredients. Mix well and chill.

Preparation Time: 10 minutes

Makes: ¾ cup

Note: A nice accompaniment to fish.

Honey Mint Dressing

1 cup oil
2 tablespoons Dijon mustard
½ cup honey
¼ cup white wine vinegar
¾ cup mayonnaise

¼ cup chopped fresh parsley
1 tablespoon chopped white onion
1 tablespoon celery seed
1 tablespoon chopped fresh mint

Combine ingredients in a blender or food processor. Blend and chill. Allow to stand for several hours for best flavor.

Preparation Time: 15 minutes

Makes: Approximately 2¾ cups

Note: Best if served the next day.

Very Special House Dressing

1 clove garlic, coarsely chopped
1 teaspoon salt
1 teaspoon Worcestershire sauce
2 tablespoons anchovy paste
3 tablespoons tarragon vinegar

3 tablespoons chopped fresh chives
⅓ cup chopped fresh parsley
1 cup mayonnaise
½ cup sour cream
½ teaspoon curry powder

Combine ingredients in a blender or food processor. Blend until creamy. Refrigerate in a covered container until ready to use.

Preparation Time: 15 minutes

Makes: Approximately 2 cups

Note: This dressing is wonderful as a dip for vegetables as well as a salad dressing. Keeps for several weeks in the refrigerator.

Apricot Chutney Dressing

¼ cup tarragon vinegar

¼ cup oil

3 tablespoons Apricot Chutney, finely
chopped (recipe page 189)

2 teaspoons sugar

1 teaspoon curry powder

¼ teaspoon salt

Combine ingredients and blend well. Refrigerate until ready to use.

Preparation Time: 10 minutes

Makes: Approximately ¾ cup

Orange Poppy Seed Dressing

½ cup oil

⅓ cup thawed orange juice
concentrate

3 tablespoons honey

2 tablespoons vinegar

1 teaspoon poppy seed

Combine ingredients in a covered container and shake well. Refrigerate until ready to use.

Preparation Time: 10 minutes

Makes: 1¼ cups

Note: Enhances a fresh fruit salad.

Breads

Hazelnut Maple Muffins with Maple Butter Glaze

Muffins

2 eggs
1 cup sour cream
1 cup maple syrup
1 cup flour
1 cup bran flakes cereal

1 teaspoon baking soda
½ teaspoon cinnamon
¾ cup coarsely chopped hazelnuts
¼ cup finely chopped hazelnuts, for topping

Preheat oven to 400 degrees. Oil muffin cups generously.

Beat eggs in a large bowl. Stir in sour cream and maple syrup. Add flour, bran flakes, baking soda, and cinnamon. Stir just until batter is moistened. Fold in hazelnuts. Fill muffin cups ⅔ full. Bake for 15 minutes or until a tester inserted in the center comes out clean.

Maple Butter Glaze

½ cup maple syrup
¼ cup butter

Combine maple syrup with butter in small saucepan over medium heat. Stir until butter is melted and blended. Remove muffins from pan. Place 1 teaspoon glaze into bottom of each muffin cup. Return muffins to cups upright. Drizzle the top of each muffin generously with glaze and sprinkle with finely chopped hazelnuts. Allow to sit for 15 minutes for glaze to absorb. Serve warm.

Preparation Time: 30 minutes

Cooking Time: 15 minutes

Makes: 10 to 12 muffins

Note: Both the aroma and flavor of these muffins are delicious. Muffins may be prepared ahead of time. Allow to cool completely, wrap, and freeze. Reheat in a warm oven.

Sweet Jalapeño Corn Muffins

Photograph appears with Table of Contents.

1 cup yellow cornmeal
1 cup flour
¼ cup sugar
2 teaspoons baking powder
1½ teaspoons salt
½ teaspoon baking soda

1 cup sour cream
2 eggs
¼ cup butter, melted
1 cup Jalapeño Pepper Jelly (recipe below)

Preheat oven to 425 degrees. Generously oil muffin cups.

Mix cornmeal, flour, sugar, baking powder, salt, and baking soda in a medium bowl. Stir sour cream, eggs, and butter together in a separate bowl. Add to dry ingredients and stir until evenly moistened (do not overmix or muffins will be tough). Fill muffin cups half full. Place 2 tablespoons Jalapeño Pepper Jelly on batter and spread barely to edges. Top with batter to fill muffin cups almost to top. Bake for 15 to 20 minutes until muffins are light golden and a tester inserted in the center comes out clean. Cool in pans for 5 minutes before removing.

Preparation Time: 20 minutes

Cooking Time: 20 minutes

Makes: 10 to 12

Jalapeño Pepper Jelly

½ cup chopped green bell pepper
¼ cup jalapeño peppers, rinsed and seeded
1¼ cups cider vinegar
6 cups sugar

½ cup diced red bell pepper
1 bottle fruit pectin
8 drops green food coloring
Canning jars and lids

Place green bell pepper and jalapeños in a food processor or blender with half of the vinegar. Blend. Pour into a 4-quart saucepan. Stir in remaining vinegar, sugar, and red bell pepper. Bring to a hard boil. Remove from heat. Allow to stand for 5 minutes. Skim foam from top. Add pectin and food coloring. Stir until blended. Pour into jars. Top with lids and invert for a better seal. Allow to cool. Refrigerate after opening.

Preparation Time: 20 minutes

Cooking Time: 10 to 15 minutes

Makes: 7 half pints

Pumpkin Pecan Muffins

¾ cup brown sugar
¼ cup dark molasses
½ cup butter, softened
1 egg, beaten
1 cup mashed pumpkin
1¾ cups flour
1 teaspoon baking soda

¼ teaspoon salt
1 teaspoon cinnamon
½ teaspoon ground nutmeg
½ teaspoon ground allspice
½ teaspoon ground ginger
¼ teaspoon ground cloves
¾ cup whole pecans

Preheat oven to 375 degrees. Oil muffin cups generously.

Cream sugar, molasses, and butter. Add egg and pumpkin, blending well. Combine flour, baking soda, salt, and spices together. Add to pumpkin mixture. Fold in pecans. Fill prepared muffin cups ⅔ full with batter. Bake for 20 minutes or until a tester inserted in the center comes out clean.

Preparation Time: 20 minutes

Cooking Time: 20 minutes

Makes: 1 dozen

Peanut Butter Bran Muffins

1 cup unbleached flour
½ cup light brown sugar, packed
1 tablespoon baking powder
¼ teaspoon salt
2 cups 40% Bran Flakes cereal

1¼ cups milk
1 egg
⅓ cup oil
⅓ to ½ cup peanut butter, plain or crunchy

Preheat oven to 400 degrees. Oil muffin cups generously.

Combine flour, sugar, baking powder, and salt in 1 bowl. Set aside. Combine cereal and milk in another bowl (do not stir). Allow cereal to stand for 3 minutes, then stir cereal into milk. Blend egg, oil, and peanut butter in another bowl. Add to cereal mixture. Add flour mixture to cereal mixture (batter will be thick). Spoon batter into prepared muffin cups. Bake for 25 minutes or until muffins are golden brown.

Preparation Time: 20 minutes

Cooking Time: 25 minutes

Makes: 1 dozen

Apple Bran Muffins

1 cup brown sugar
¾ teaspoon salt
2 teaspoons baking soda
2 teaspoons baking powder
2½ cups bran
1½ cups oats
1 cup flour
1⅓ cups whole wheat flour
½ teaspoon cinnamon
¼ teaspoon ground nutmeg
⅔ cup oil
½ cup honey

¼ cup molasses
1 teaspoon vanilla
4 eggs
16 ounces plain yogurt
1 cup buttermilk
½ cup applesauce
¼ cup apple cider
½ cup diced dried apples
½ cup raisins
½ cup chopped walnuts
1 teaspoon grated lemon peel

Combine brown sugar, salt, baking soda, baking powder, bran, oats, flour, whole wheat flour, cinnamon, and nutmeg in a large bowl. Set aside. Combine remaining ingredients. Blend well. Fold yogurt mixture gently into flour mixture until dry ingredients are moistened (do not overmix). Cover and refrigerate overnight.

Preheat oven to 400 degrees. Oil muffin cups generously.

Pour batter into prepared muffin cups. Bake for 25 to 30 minutes.

Preparation Time: 8 hours (includes refrigerating batter overnight)
Cooking Time: 30 minutes
Makes: 1 dozen

Gingered Orange Muffins

6 tablespoons butter, softened
1½ cups sugar
1 egg
½ cup sour cream
½ teaspoon orange extract
1¼ cups flour

½ teaspoon baking soda
½ teaspoon salt
1 teaspoon ground ginger
¾ cup chopped pecans
3 tablespoons grated orange peel
3 tablespoons orange juice

Preheat oven to 375 degrees. Oil muffin cups generously.

Cream butter with sugar. Beat in egg. Add sour cream and orange extract and blend. Set aside. Combine flour, baking soda, salt, and ginger. Add to butter mixture and blend. Add pecans, orange peel, and orange juice and mix well. Spoon into prepared muffin cups, filling ⅔ full. Bake for 25 minutes or until a tester inserted in the center comes out clean.

Preparation Time: 20 minutes
Cooking Time: 25 minutes
Makes: 10 to 12

Note: May use a mini muffin pan. If so, bake for 15 to 18 minutes. Makes 3 dozen.

Orange Poppy Seed Muffins

1¼ cups flour
¾ cup sugar
¼ teaspoon salt
⅓ cup poppy seed
2 teaspoons baking powder
1 egg

½ cup milk
⅓ cup oil
½ teaspoon orange extract
¼ cup freshly squeezed orange juice
2 tablespoons orange zest

Preheat oven to 375 degrees. Oil muffin cups generously.

Combine flour, sugar, salt, poppy seed, and baking powder. Beat in egg. Combine milk, oil, orange extract, and orange juice in another bowl. Add orange zest. Add wet ingredients to flour mixture and blend until smooth. Fill prepared muffin cups ⅔ full. Bake for 20 minutes or until golden. Cool on a wire rack.

Preparation Time: 20 minutes

Cooking Time: 15 to 20 minutes

Makes: 1 dozen

Gorgonzola Herb Bread

6 ounces Gorgonzola cheese,
   softened
12 ounces cream cheese, softened
½ teaspoon dried basil
½ teaspoon dried parsley

½ teaspoon dried oregano
½ teaspoon dried chervil
½ teaspoon summer savory
1 long baguette (French bread)
¼ cup butter, softened

Cream the cheeses until fluffy. Place mixture in a serving dish. Set aside.

Combine herbs. Slice baguette in half lengthwise with 1 long cut. Spread with butter. Sprinkle herbs over top and broil until lightly browned. Cut bread into wedges and serve warm with the cheese spread on the side (cheese spread should be at room temperature).

Preparation Time: 15 minutes

Cooking Time: 2 to 3 minutes

Serves: 6 to 8

Note: Blue cheese may be substituted for Gorgonzola.

Savory Herb Pinwheels

Proofing is the process of testing the freshness of the yeast.

1 teaspoon active dry yeast
2 tablespoons warm water (105 to 115 degrees)
2 tablespoons plus pinch sugar
½ cup vegetable shortening
1 teaspoon salt
½ cup hot water
1 egg
½ cup cold water

3 cups flour
1 cup butter, softened
⅓ cup minced fresh parsley
⅓ cup minced fresh Italian parsley
½ cup minced green onions
1 tablespoon minced chives
2 teaspoons dry mustard
¼ teaspoon salt

Proof the yeast in warm water with a pinch of sugar for 15 minutes or until foamy (if it does not foam, it will not allow bread to rise). Cream the shortening, sugar, and salt together with an electric mixer. Add the hot water slowly while beating and beat for 1 minute. Beat the egg with the cold water in a separate bowl and stir in the yeast mixture. Add the egg mixture slowly to the shortening mixture while beating. Beat for 5 minutes. Beat in the flour ½ cup at a time. Beat the dough until it is smooth. Cover the dough and chill for a minimum of 4 hours or overnight (the dough will not rise).

Cream the butter in a small bowl. Add both parsleys, green onions, chives, dry mustard, and salt. Blend well. Set aside, reserving ¼ cup for top.

Form half of the dough into a ball and roll it out into a 12 × 8-inch rectangle on a lightly floured surface and with floured hands. Spread half of the herb butter over the dough in a thin layer. Roll up the dough in a jelly roll fashion, starting with the long side. Repeat this process for the second ball of dough and remaining herb butter. At this point, the rolls and ¼ cup reserved herb butter may be kept in the refrigerator for up to 1 week wrapped in plastic wrap.

Preheat oven to 375 degrees. Oil muffin cups generously.

Cut each roll into 10 to 12 pieces. Place rolls, cut side up, in prepared muffin cups and bake for 20 to 30 minutes or until golden. Brush tops with the remaining softened herb butter while they are still hot. Serve in a napkin-lined basket.

Preparation Time: 5 hours (includes resting time for dough)
Cooking Time: 20 to 30 minutes
Makes: 20 to 24

Tomato Fennel Bread; Zesty Butter Sticks; Soft Bavarian Pretzels; Savory Herb Pinwheels.

Tomato Fennel Bread

2 packages active dry yeast
1½ cups warm water (105 to 115 degrees)
2 tablespoons sugar
2 teaspoons salt

2 tablespoons olive oil
2 teaspoons fennel seed
4½ cups flour
½ cup tomato paste
Olive oil to serve

Sprinkle yeast over warm water in a large bowl, stirring until dissolved. Add sugar, salt, olive oil, fennel seed, and 3 cups flour. Beat until blended. Add tomato paste and blend well. Add remaining flour gradually, stirring well. Rub olive oil over dough. Cover with wax paper and a towel. Allow to rise in a warm place (about 85 degrees) until doubled in size, about 45 minutes.

Preheat oven to 375 degrees. Oil a 9-inch pie plate lightly.

Stir down dough after it has risen. Beat with a wooden spoon for 30 seconds. Turn dough into prepared pie plate or onto an oiled baking sheet and shape into a mound. Rub dough with olive oil. Bake for 50 minutes or until browned. Cool on a wire rack. Serve with olive oil for dipping.

Preparation Time: 1 hour (includes rising time)
Cooking Time: 50 minutes
Makes: 1 loaf

Note: Dipping chunks of this wonderful bread in olive oil is a great alternative to butter and enhances the tomato fennel flavor of the bread.

Zesty Butter Sticks

1 loaf French bread, uncut
1 cup butter, softened
1 teaspoon dried chervil
1 teaspoon dried basil leaves

½ teaspoon dried oregano leaves
1 teaspoon garlic powder
½ teaspoon onion powder

Preheat oven to 425 degrees.

Cut bread into 6-inch long thin bread sticks. Combine remaining ingredients in a medium bowl. Blend well. Spread butter mixture on all surfaces of the bread sticks. Bake for 7 to 8 minutes or until golden.

Preparation Time: 10 minutes

Cooking Time: 7 to 8 minutes

Serves: 8

Soft Bavarian Pretzels

1½ teaspoons active dry yeast
¾ cup lukewarm water (105 to 115 degrees)
½ teaspoon salt

¼ teaspoon sugar
2 cups flour
1 egg, beaten
Coarse salt

Preheat oven to 450 degrees.

Soften yeast in water. Add salt and sugar. Mix in flour and knead into a smooth dough (do not allow mixture to rise). Cut dough into pieces and roll into pretzel shapes. Cover a baking sheet with foil and dust with flour. Lay pretzels on prepared baking sheet. Brush pretzels with beaten egg and sprinkle with coarse salt. Bake for 15 minutes or until golden.

Preparation Time: 20 minutes

Cooking Time: 15 minutes

Makes: 10 to 12

Note: If coarse salt is unavailable, margarita or kosher salt works well.

Swiss Cheese Puff

1 cup milk
¼ cup butter
½ teaspoon salt
¼ teaspoon pepper

1 cup flour
4 eggs, room temperature
⅔ pound Swiss cheese, diced

Preheat oven to 375 degrees. Oil a 9-inch pie plate generously.

Bring milk and butter to a boil in a medium saucepan. Add salt and pepper. Remove from heat. Add flour. Stir until smooth. Add eggs 1 at a time, mixing well after each addition. Stir cheese into batter. Spoon batter into prepared pie plate. Bake until golden brown, about 45 minutes.

Preparation Time: 15 minutes

Cooking Time: 45 minutes

Serves: 6 to 8

Note: Bread puffs similar to a soufflé, therefore, serve immediately.

Parmesan Herb Bread

2 tablespoons active dry yeast
2 cups warm water (105 degrees to 115 degrees)
2 tablespoons sugar
2 teaspoons salt
2 tablespoons butter, softened

½ cup plus 1 tablespoon freshly grated Parmesan cheese
1½ tablespoons dried oregano leaves
4½ cups flour, sifted before measuring

Sprinkle yeast over water in a large bowl, stirring until dissolved. Add sugar, salt, butter, ½ cup Parmesan cheese, oregano, and 3 cups flour. Beat at low speed until blended. Beat 2 minutes at medium speed until smooth, scraping down sides of bowl periodically with wooden spoon. Beat in remaining flour gradually with a wooden spoon. Cover with wax paper and a towel. Allow dough to rise in a warm place (85 degrees) until light, bubbly, and more than double in bulk, about 45 minutes.

Preheat oven to 375 degrees. Oil a 1½ to 2-quart casserole lightly.

Stir down batter using a wooden spoon and beat vigorously for 30 seconds. Turn into prepared dish. Sprinkle with 1 tablespoon Parmesan cheese. Bake for 50 to 55 minutes or until nicely browned. Allow to cool for 5 minutes on wire rack before cutting.

Preparation Time: 15 minutes
Cooking Time: 50 to 55 minutes
Makes: 1 loaf

Popovers

3 eggs
1 cup flour
1 cup milk

¼ teaspoon salt
1 tablespoon oil

Combine ingredients, in the order written, in a blender until frothy. Oil 6 large popover or 6 4-ounce size Pyrex custard cups generously. Pour batter into prepared cups, filling ¾ full. Bake at 375 degrees in a *non*-preheated oven for 40 to 45 minutes. Bake until browned.

Preparation Time: 10 minutes

Cooking Time: 40 to 45 minutes

Makes: 6 large popovers

Note: Once cooled, popovers may be kept in a sealed plastic bag. Re-crisp in a 375 degree oven for 5 minutes. Grated Gruyère, Cheddar, or Parmesan cheese may be added to offer a new twist to an old favorite (use 1 tablespoon of cheese per popover). For more flavor variety, see recipes pages 129, 132, and 135.

Country Skillet Cornbread

6 strips bacon
½ cup flour
1¼ cups yellow cornmeal
1 tablespoon baking powder
1 teaspoon salt
2 eggs, beaten
1½ cups milk
½ cup oil

½ cup sour cream
1 cup fresh corn (approximately 1 ear)
1 medium onion, chopped
1 cup shredded sharp Cheddar cheese
2 jalapeño peppers, seeded and diced or 3½ ounces diced green chiles

Preheat oven to 350 degrees. Oil a 10-inch cast iron skillet or an ovenproof pan. Place pan in oven to heat.

Cook bacon until crisp. Drain, crumble, and set aside. Sift flour, cornmeal, baking powder, and salt together. Set aside. Combine remaining ingredients and bacon in another bowl. Add to dry ingredients and blend well. Pour into the hot skillet. Bake for 30 to 40 minutes or until golden on top. Allow to cool for 5 to 10 minutes before cutting.

Preparation Time: 30 minutes
Cooking Time: 30 to 40 minutes
Serves: 6 to 8

Note: May be made in a 10×10-inch baking dish. May add more peppers for additional flavor.

Buttermilk Scones

A scone is a Scottish biscuit shaped into squares, rounds, or triangles and baked or deep fried.

4 cups buttermilk
2 tablespoons active dry yeast
¼ cup warm water (105 to 115 degrees)
¼ cup sugar
2 eggs, beaten
2 tablespoons oil
1½ teaspoons salt
1 tablespoon baking powder

1 teaspoon baking soda
8 cups flour
Oil for frying
Cinnamon-sugar for garnish
Honey to serve
Butter to serve
Jam to serve

Heat buttermilk until warm. Soften yeast in water. Combine buttermilk, sugar, eggs, oil, salt, baking powder, baking soda, and 4 cups flour. Add yeast. Beat until smooth. Add remaining flour and blend to a soft dough. Coat a mixing bowl with a thin layer of oil. Form dough into a ball and roll it in the oil-coated bowl to cover evenly with oil. Cover and set aside, allowing dough to rise until it has doubled in size. Punch down slightly and knead dough for 1 minute. Replace in bowl. Cover and refrigerate overnight.

Heat oil in a large skillet to 375 degrees. Roll out dough on a floured board until ¼-inch thick. Cut into 2-inch squares. Stretch out squares slightly before frying. Fry on 1 side until golden brown. Turn and fry other side until golden brown. Drain on paper towels. Sprinkle with cinnamon-sugar. Serve hot with honey, butter, or jam.

Preparation Time: 2 hours
Makes: 60 to 80

Note: Dough will keep refrigerated for 3 to 4 days. Keep punching down and keep tightly covered.

Pain d'Orange

1 medium orange	1 teaspoon salt
1 cup dates	1 cup sugar
1 cup raisins	2 tablespoons butter, melted
Boiling water	1 egg, beaten
2 cups flour	1 teaspoon vanilla
1 teaspoon baking powder	½ cup chopped walnuts
1 teaspoon baking soda	

Preheat oven to 350 degrees. Oil and flour a 9 × 5-inch loaf pan.

Squeeze the juice from the orange and set aside. Separate the white pith from the rind and discard the pith. Grind orange rind, dates, and raisins in a food processor. Set aside. Measure orange juice into an 8-ounce measuring cup. Add enough boiling water to make 1 cup. Sift flour, baking powder, baking soda, and salt together. Set aside. Combine orange rind mixture, the diluted orange juice, sugar, butter, egg, and vanilla. Gradually add to dry ingredients and nuts. Mix until just blended. Pour into prepared loaf pan and bake for 1 hour.

Preparation Time: 25 minutes

Cooking Time: 1 hour

Makes: 1 loaf

Cranberry Orange Bread

2 cups plus 1 teaspoon flour
½ teaspoon salt
1½ teaspoons baking powder
½ teaspoon baking soda
1 cup sugar
Grated rind and juice of 1 orange

2 tablespoons oil
Water
1 egg, beaten
1 cup chopped walnuts
1 cup fresh cranberries

Preheat oven to 325 degrees. Oil a 9 × 5-inch loaf pan.

Sift together 2 cups flour, salt, baking powder, and baking soda. Add sugar. Set aside. Combine grated rind, orange juice, oil, and enough boiling water to make ¾ cup liquid. Add orange mixture and the beaten egg to the dry mixture. Add nuts and blend. Cut each cranberry in half and toss lightly with the remaining 1 teaspoon flour. Fold cranberries gently into batter. Pour into prepared pan. Bake for 1 hour or until a tester inserted in the center comes out clean.

Preparation Time: 15 minutes
Cooking Time: 1 hour
Makes: 1 loaf

Sausage Bread

1 cup raisins

Water

1 pound hot bulk sausage, uncooked

1½ cups brown sugar

1½ cups white sugar

3 eggs

1 cup pecans

3 cups flour

1 teaspoon ground ginger

1 teaspoon pumpkin pie spice

1 teaspoon baking powder

1 teaspoon baking soda

1 cup cold coffee

Preheat oven to 350 degrees. Oil and flour a 9-inch tube pan or 2 9×5-inch loaf pans.

Simmer raisins in a saucepan with enough water to cover for 5 minutes. Drain. Mix uncooked sausage with sugars and eggs. Stir in nuts and raisins. Set aside. Mix flour, spices, and baking powder together. Set aside. Stir baking soda into coffee. Add flour mixture and coffee to sausage mixture. Blend well. Pour into prepared pan(s). Bake for 1 hour.

Preparation Time: 15 minutes

Cooking Time: 1 hour

Serves: 8 to 10

Apple Raisin Bread

2 cups flour
1 teaspoon baking powder
½ teaspoon baking soda
½ teaspoon salt
⅓ cup butter, softened
1 cup sugar
1 egg

⅓ cup orange juice
½ teaspoon cinnamon
¾ cup raisins
½ cup chopped walnuts
1 cup chopped apple
1 tablespoon grated orange peel

Preheat oven to 350 degrees. Oil a 9×5-inch loaf pan.

Sift together flour, baking powder, baking soda, and salt. Set aside. Cream butter, gradually adding sugar. Add egg and mix. Add flour mixture and orange juice alternately to butter mixture, blending well after each addition. Stir in cinnamon, raisins, nuts, apple, and orange peel. Pour into prepared pan. Bake for 50 minutes to 1 hour.

Preparation Time: 15 minutes
Cooking Time: 50 minutes to 1 hour
Makes: 1 loaf

Note: Freezes well. Pecans may be substituted for walnuts.

Caribbean Banana Nut Bread

1 cup whole wheat flour
1 cup unbleached flour
1 teaspoon baking soda
½ teaspoon salt
½ cup butter
1 cup raw sugar
2 eggs

1½ cups mashed ripe bananas
⅓ cup milk
1 teaspoon lemon juice
1 teaspoon rum extract
1 cup chopped macadamia nuts
¾ cup shredded coconut

Preheat oven to 350 degrees. Oil a 9 × 5-inch loaf pan.

Combine flours, baking soda, and salt. Set aside. Cream butter and sugar. Add eggs and bananas. Blend well. Add milk, lemon juice, and rum extract and blend well. Add dry ingredients, a little at a time, mixing well after each addition. Fold in nuts and coconut. Pour into prepared pan. Bake for 1 hour to 1 hour 10 minutes or until a tester inserted in the center comes out clean.

Preparation Time: 20 minutes
Cooking Time: 1 hour to 1 hour 10 minutes
Makes: 1 loaf

Note: The ever favorite banana nut bread with a tropical twist. Best if served the next day. Should be kept in the refrigerator.

Carrot Bread

2 eggs
1 cup sugar
⅔ cup oil
1½ cups flour
¾ teaspoon baking soda
1 teaspoon cinnamon

1 teaspoon ground nutmeg
½ teaspoon salt
1½ cups grated carrots
1 cup chopped walnuts
¾ cup raisins

Preheat oven to 350 degrees. Oil a 9×5-inch loaf pan.

Beat eggs. Add sugar and oil. Sift together flour, baking soda, cinnamon, nutmeg, and salt. Add to egg mixture. Beat well. Fold in carrots, nuts, and raisins. Pour batter into prepared pan. Bake for 55 minutes to 1 hour.

Preparation Time: 15 minutes
Cooking Time: 55 minutes to 1 hour
Makes: 1 loaf

Apple Nut Brunch Cake

½ cup plus 1 tablespoon butter
1 cup sugar
2 eggs
1 teaspoon vanilla
1 cup sour cream
2 cups flour
1 teaspoon baking powder

1 teaspoon baking soda
¼ teaspoon salt
2 cups finely chopped apple
½ cup chopped walnuts
½ cup brown sugar
2 teaspoons cinnamon

Preheat oven to 350 degrees. Oil a 9×13-inch pan.

Cream ½ cup butter and sugar. Add eggs, vanilla, and sour cream. Blend well. Set aside. Sift together flour, baking powder, baking soda, and salt. Add to creamed mixture. Fold in apple. Spread batter into prepared pan. Combine nuts, brown sugar, cinnamon, and 1 tablespoon melted butter. Blend until coarse. Sprinkle mixture over batter. Bake for 35 to 40 minutes.

Preparation Time: 15 minutes
Cooking Time: 40 minutes
Serves: 8 to 10

Chocolate Chip Bourbon Pecan Loaf

2 cups flour

1 teaspoon baking powder

¾ teaspoon baking soda

½ teaspoon salt

2 eggs

½ cup butter, softened

½ cup pure maple syrup

⅓ cup dark brown sugar, packed

½ cup buttermilk

½ cup chocolate chips

1 cup coarsely chopped pecans

5 tablespoons bourbon

Preheat oven to 350 degrees. Oil 9 × 5-inch loaf pan.

Combine flour, baking powder, baking soda, and salt. Set aside. Beat eggs, butter, syrup, and sugar together at medium speed until light and fluffy. Reduce speed to low. Add flour mixture and buttermilk alternately to egg mixture, beating well after each addition. Stir in chocolate chips, pecans, and bourbon. Pour into prepared pan, smoothing top. Bake for 50 minutes to 1 hour or until a tester inserted in the center comes out clean. Allow to cool in pan on a wire rack for 10 minutes. Remove loaf from pan and cool completely on a wire rack. Store in a sealed plastic bag or airtight container.

Preparation Time: 30 minutes

Cooking Time: 50 minutes to 1 hour

Makes: 1 loaf

Note: This wonderfully rich bread may be served as a dessert. It is best served the day after it is made.

Cinnamon Pecan Coffee Cake

2 cups chopped pecans, toasted
2 tablespoons sugar
1 tablespoon cinnamon
1 cup butter, softened
2 cups sugar
2 eggs

1 cup sour cream
2 teaspoons vanilla
2 cups flour
½ teaspoon baking powder
¼ teaspoon salt
Powdered sugar

Preheat oven to 350 degrees. Oil and flour a 9-inch bundt pan.

Combine pecans, sugar, and cinnamon. Set aside. Cream butter and sugar at high speed until light and fluffy. Blend in eggs 1 at a time. Stir in sour cream and vanilla. Set aside. Combine flour, baking powder, and salt. Mix well. Fold into butter mixture. Pour a third of the batter into the prepared pan and smooth. Sprinkle half of the nut mixture on top. Pour in a third more batter and smooth. Sprinkle remaining nut mixture on top. Add remaining batter. Bake for 1 hour to 1 hour 15 minutes. Cool in pan for 5 minutes. Invert onto a platter and allow to cool for about 30 minutes. Dust generously with powdered sugar.

Preparation Time: 30 minutes
Cooking Time: 1 hour to 1 hour 15 minutes
Serves: 10

Chocolate Chip Coffee Cake

Topping

¼ cup white sugar

⅓ cup brown sugar

1 teaspoon cinnamon

1 cup chopped walnuts

6 ounces chocolate chips

Combine topping ingredients and set aside.

Batter

½ cup butter, softened

1 cup sugar

2 eggs

1 cup sour cream

1 teaspoon baking powder

1 teaspoon baking soda

1 teaspoon salt

2 teaspoons vanilla

2 cups sifted flour

Preheat oven to 350 degrees. Oil a 9-inch bundt pan.

Cream butter and sugar. Beat until smooth. Add eggs and sour cream and blend. Add baking powder, baking soda, salt, and vanilla. Mix well. Add flour slowly and beat until smooth. Sprinkle a third of the topping mixture into bottom of prepared pan. Spoon half of the batter over the topping. Sprinkle another third of the topping over the layer of batter. Spoon in remaining batter and sprinkle with the remaining topping mixture. Bake for 45 minutes or until a tester inserted in the center comes out clean.

Preparation Time: 25 minutes

Cooking Time: 45 minutes

Makes: 1 cake

Note: A great way to satisfy the chocolate lover's sweet tooth early in the day.

Brunch

Spiced Pumpkin Pancakes with Sautéed Apples

½ cup yellow cornmeal
½ cup unbleached flour
1 teaspoon baking powder
¼ cup brown sugar
½ teaspoon ground ginger
¼ teaspoon ground allspice
½ teaspoon cinnamon
Pinch nutmeg
Salt
1 teaspoon grated orange or lemon zest

1 egg
½ cup mashed pumpkin
½ cup milk
4 tablespoons butter
2 large sweet apples, peeled, cored, and thinly sliced (Red or Golden Delicious or Rome Beauties are suggested)
Maple syrup to serve
Chopped pecans to serve

Sift dry ingredients together. Add the citrus zest, egg, pumpkin, and milk. Beat to a smooth batter.

Melt butter and sauté apple slices until golden and just tender. Set aside and keep hot.

Heat a lightly oiled griddle or skillet over medium heat and pour batter onto surface. Cook until bubbles appear at the edges. Turn and cook until golden and just firm to the touch. Keep warm while making remaining pancakes. Serve with the apples, maple syrup, and chopped pecans.

Preparation Time: 30 minutes

Cooking Time: 30 minutes

Serves: 4

Note: Fragrant and delicious autumn brunch.

Apple Pancake

5 medium tart apples, peeled, cored,
   and thinly sliced
Butter
½ cup milk
½ cup flour
3 eggs

1 teaspoon sugar
Salt
Powdered sugar
Cinnamon
Lemon juice (optional)

Preheat oven to 500 degrees.

Sauté apple slices in butter in an ovenproof skillet until tender but firm. Mix milk, flour, eggs, sugar, and salt together. Add to apples and toss. Place skillet in oven for 8 minutes. Remove and sprinkle with powdered sugar and cinnamon. Dot with butter and return to oven for 3 to 4 minutes until golden and butter is melted. Sprinkle with lemon juice just before serving, if desired. Allow to cool for 30 seconds to 1 minute before serving.

Preparation Time: 30 minutes

Cooking Time: 12 minutes

Serves: 4 to 6

Spinach Popovers

3 eggs
1 cup flour
1 cup milk
¼ teaspoon salt

1 tablespoon oil
½ cup fresh spinach leaves, packed
¼ teaspoon ground nutmeg

Combine ingredients in a blender in the order written. Blend until frothy. Generously oil 6 popover cups or 6 4-ounce size Pyrex custard cups. Pour batter into prepared cups, filling ¾ full. Bake at 375 degrees in a *non*-preheated oven for 40 to 45 minutes. Bake until browned.

Preparation Time: 10 minutes

Cooking Time: 40 to 45 minutes

Makes: 6

Note: Once cooled, the popovers may be kept in a sealed plastic bag overnight. Recrisp in a 375 degree oven for 5 minutes.

Vegetable Garden Pancakes

1 cup finely chopped onion
¼ cup finely chopped green bell pepper
½ cup finely chopped celery
1½ cups grated carrots
3 tablespoons butter
1 package chopped spinach, thawed, drained, and patted dry
3 eggs, beaten

¾ cup bread crumbs
1½ teaspoons salt
¼ teaspoon pepper
Oil
Sour cream to serve
Chopped tomato to serve
Chopped fresh parsley for garnish

Sauté onion, green pepper, celery, and carrots in butter for 10 minutes. Add spinach. Set aside. Combine eggs with bread crumbs, salt, and pepper. Add to spinach mixture. Refrigerate for at least 15 minutes. Form pancakes (small for appetizer, larger for side dish or entrée). Sauté pancakes in ¼-inch hot oil until golden. Turn and brown on other side. Drain on paper towels. Serve with sour cream and chopped tomato. Garnish with parsley.

Preparation Time: 15 minutes

Cooking Time: 10 minutes

Makes: 12 appetizers

8 side dishes or entrées

Note: May be frozen. Reheat at 350 degrees for 10 minutes.

Three Grain Buttermilk Pancakes

2 cups buttermilk

2 teaspoons baking soda

½ cup sour cream

2 eggs

½ cup uncooked oatmeal

½ teaspoon salt

1 cup flour

¼ cup sugar

¾ teaspoon baking powder

¼ cup corn flour

Oil

Butter to serve

Syrup to serve

Combine buttermilk, baking soda, and sour cream. Stir until foaming stops, about 3 minutes. Add remaining ingredients except oil and blend.

Heat oil in a large skillet or griddle. Pour about ¼ cup of batter for each pancake onto the griddle. Cook until bubbles appear around the edges. Turn and cook for another 20 to 30 seconds or until golden. Serve with butter and syrup of choice.

Preparation Time: 15 minutes

Cooking Time: Approximately 1½ minutes

Serves: 4

Note: This mixture will keep in the refrigerator for several weeks. For variation, add sliced banana or fresh blueberries and chopped nuts while cooking.

Pesto Popovers

3 eggs	**1 tablespoon olive oil**
1 cup flour	**⅓ cup Parmesan cheese**
1 cup milk	**¼ cup fresh basil, packed**
¼ teaspoon salt	**¼ teaspoon garlic powder**

Combine ingredients in a blender in the order written. Blend until frothy. Generously oil 6 popover cups or 6 4-ounce size Pyrex custard cups. Pour batter into prepared cups, filling ¾ full. Bake at 375 degrees in a *non*-preheated oven for 40 to 45 minutes. Bake until browned.

Preparation Time: 10 minutes

Cooking Time: 40 to 45 minutes

Makes: 6

Note: Once cooled, the popovers may be kept in a sealed plastic bag overnight. Recrisp in a 375 degree oven for 5 minutes.

Chocolate Orange Popovers

3 eggs	**1 tablespoon oil**
1 cup flour	**1 tablespoon cocoa**
1 cup milk	**1 tablespoon sugar**
¼ teaspoon salt	**1 tablespoon grated orange peel**

Combine ingredients in a blender in the order written. Blend until frothy. Generously oil 6 popover cups or 6 4-ounce size Pyrex custard cups. Pour batter into prepared cups, filling ¾ full. Bake at 375 degrees in a *non*-preheated oven for 40 to 45 minutes. Bake until browned.

Preparation Time: 10 minutes

Cooking Time: 40 to 45 minutes

Makes: 6

Note: Once cooled, the popovers may be kept in a sealed plastic bag overnight. Recrisp in a 375 degree oven for 5 minutes.

Crispy Cinnamon Logs

Cinnamon Logs

1 pound loaf of unsliced or thick
  sliced white bread, crusts trimmed
  (may use sourdough)
2 cups milk
5 eggs, beaten
2 tablespoons sugar
1 teaspoon cinnamon
½ teaspoon vanilla

¼ teaspoon mace
Oil
Powdered sugar for garnish
Cinnamon Maple Syrup to serve
  (recipe below)
Three Berry Sauce to serve (recipe
  page 204)

Cut bread into 4×2×2-inch logs. Allow to stand to dry slightly. Combine milk, eggs, sugar, cinnamon, vanilla, and mace. Pour egg mixture into a pan large enough to hold logs in 1 layer. Arrange logs in egg mixture, turning to coat all sides. Cover with plastic wrap and refrigerate until all liquid is absorbed, for several hours or overnight.

Heat oil in a large skillet. Fry logs until golden and crispy on all sides. Drain on paper towels. Sift powdered sugar over logs and serve with warm Cinnamon Maple Syrup or Three Berry Sauce.

Cinnamon Maple Syrup

4 cups sugar
¼ cup brown sugar
½ cup water

¼ teaspoon maple flavoring
¼ teaspoon vanilla
2 sticks cinnamon

Boil sugars and water for 10 minutes. Cool. Add maple flavoring, vanilla, and cinnamon sticks. Simmer over low heat for 10 to 15 minutes.

Preparation Time: 25 minutes

Cooking Time: 25 to 35 minutes

Serves: 6

Layered Tricolor Pasta Frittata

¼ pound spinach fettucini
¼ pound egg fettucini
6 tablespoons olive oil
Salt
Pepper
1 cup freshly grated Parmesan cheese
1 cup freshly grated Romano cheese
½ cup finely chopped onion
2 cloves garlic, minced

28 ounces canned peeled Italian plum tomatoes, chopped plus ½ cup of the liquid
1 cup diced mozzarella cheese
½ cup pine nuts
½ cup chopped fresh basil
¼ cup golden raisins
6 eggs
¼ cup light cream
¼ cup chopped fresh Italian parsley

Cook fettucini according to package directions until tender but firm (al dente). Drain. Toss with 2 tablespoons olive oil and season with salt and pepper in a large bowl. Set aside and cool completely.

Combine Parmesan and Romano cheeses and set aside.

Heat 3 tablespoons olive oil in a large skillet. Sauté onion and garlic until tender, stirring occasionally. Increase heat to medium high. Add tomatoes and the ½ cup of liquid. Cook until mixture is thick, stirring frequently, for about 10 to 15 minutes. Cool to room temperature. Add mozzarella cheese and 1 cup of the combined Parmesan and Romano cheeses. Season with salt and pepper.

Heat 1 tablespoon olive oil over medium heat. Add pine nuts and sauté until golden brown, about 5 minutes. Remove with a slotted spoon and drain on a paper towel. Add pine nuts, basil, and raisins to the tomato and cheese mixture.

Preheat oven to 350 degrees.

Continued on next page

Beat eggs and cream together. Stir in ¼ cup of the combined Parmesan and Romano cheeses and half of the chopped parsley. Season with salt and pepper. Toss with the pasta. Oil a shallow baking dish. Spread half of the pasta in the bottom. Spread the tomato and cheese mixture over the pasta. Top with the remaining pasta. Sprinkle with the remaining ¾ cup combined Parmesan and Romano cheeses and the remaining chopped parsley. Bake for 30 minutes or until top is golden.

Preparation Time: 1 hour
Cooking Time: 30 minutes
Serves: 8

Note: The savory blend of Italian favorites make this a delicate and light pasta dish.

Breakfast Popovers

3 eggs
1 cup flour
1 cup milk
¼ teaspoon salt

2 tablespoons butter, melted
1 cup diced Swiss cheese
1 cup diced ham

Preheat oven to 400 degrees.

Combine eggs, flour, milk, salt, and butter in the order written in a blender. Blend until frothy. Generously oil 6 large popover cups or 6 4-ounce size Pyrex cups. Place cheese and ham in cups, dividing evenly. Pour batter over top, filling cups ¾ full. Bake for 35 to 40 minutes or until browned. Remove from cups and serve immediately.

Preparation Time: 10 minutes
Cooking Time: 35 to 40 minutes
Makes: 6

Note: Batter may be prepared ahead of time and refrigerated. If using chilled batter, add 5 minutes to baking time. Once popovers are cooled, they may be kept in a sealed plastic bag overnight. Recrisp in a 375 degree oven for 5 minutes.

Asparagus Tips and Prosciutto Brioches

Blanching is a process used to improve the appearance, flavor, and tenderness of fruits and vegetables. It involves plunging them quickly into boiling water and then into cold. This process is also used to loosen the skins of fruits and vegetables for easy removal and as a preliminary step to freezing them.

Crème Fraîche
2 cups heavy cream
5 teaspoons buttermilk

Combine cream and buttermilk in a glass jar with a tight-fitting lid and shake well. Allow to stand at room temperature for about 24 hours or until thickened. Refrigerate.

Asparagus Tips and Prosciutto Brioches

6 tablespoons butter
2 shallots, minced
½ pound fresh mushrooms, diced
1 pound asparagus, blanched and cut in ¼-inch lengths
¼ teaspoon White Wine Worcestershire sauce

3 tablespoons dry vermouth
Salt
Freshly ground pepper
1½ cups Crème Fraîche
8 ounces prosciutto, julienned
8 brioches

Melt butter in a large skillet. Add shallots and sauté gently. Stir in mushrooms and sauté until tender. Add asparagus, White Wine Worcestershire sauce, vermouth, salt, and pepper. Cook on medium-high heat until liquid is reduced. Add Crème Fraîche and simmer for 5 to 7 minutes, stirring constantly. Add prosciutto. Allow sauce to thicken, then simmer for 1 minute.

Cut a thin slice off the top of each brioche, saving the lids. Hollow out the centers. Warm brioches in oven. Spoon proscuitto mixture into warmed brioche cups and top with lids to serve.

Preparation Time: 40 minutes
Cooking Time: 12 to 15 minutes
Serves: 8

Preceding pages feature: Asparagus Tips and Prosciutto Brioches; Cinnamon Pecan Coffee Cake.

Coconut Custard Brunch Cups

4 acorn squash (1 to 1¼ pounds
    each), gold or green skins
Water
1½ cups canned or thawed frozen
    coconut milk (not cream of
    coconut)

3 eggs
⅓ cup plus 2 tablespoons brown
    sugar, packed
2 teaspoons crushed anise seed
¼ cup shredded coconut

Preheat oven to 350 degrees.

Cut off ¼ of the stem end of the squash to make the lid. Remove seeds from squash and stem end (lid) and discard seeds. Hollow out enough of the squash flesh so each squash will hold ¾ cup of water. Discard water after measuring. Cut off just enough of the pointed end of each squash so each will sit level. Sit squash cups upright in a shallow baking dish large enough to hold squash side by side. Set lids on squash. Add ½-inch water to pan. Bake squash with lids on top, uncovered, for 15 minutes.

Whisk together coconut milk, eggs, and ⅓ cup brown sugar. Fill squash cups with egg mixture and set lids on top. Bake for 1 hour 30 minutes or until squash is soft when pierced and custard is firm when jiggled (lift off lids to check).

Preheat broiler.

Remove lids. Sprinkle custard cups with crushed anise seed, remaining 2 tablespoons brown sugar, and shredded coconut. Place under broiler without the lids and broil until coconut is toasted and brown sugar is bubbly (be careful not to let it burn). Replace lids on top for serving.

Preparation Time: 45 minutes
Cooking Time: 1 hour 30 minutes
Serves: 4

Note: The squash may be prepared up to the point prior to filling with custard and kept in the refrigerator for up to 2 days with lids on. Bring to room temperature before using. The combination of the creamy coconut custard in the nutty acorn squash is a unique and delightful brunch dish. Serve with crisp bacon and a warm loaf of Caribbean Banana Nut Bread (recipe page 121).

Pesto Cream with Sun Dried Tomatoes

Pesto is a thick paste-like sauce of olive oil, garlic, fresh basil, pine nuts, and Parmesan cheese. It is usually served with pasta or as a flavor enhancer to soups and sauces.

1½ ounces sun dried tomatoes
Water
1 cup fresh basil leaves, packed
½ cup pine nuts
4 large cloves garlic
¾ cup grated Parmesan cheese
½ cup olive oil
½ cup heavy cream

½ cup dry white wine
Salt
Pepper
2 ripe but firm tomatoes, chopped
Pasta Fresca to serve (recipe page 141)
Crusty sourdough bread to serve

Soak sun dried tomatoes in enough water to cover for 30 minutes. Prepare pesto by placing basil, pine nuts, garlic, and Parmesan cheese in a food processor. Process until coarse. Pour olive oil slowly down tube with motor running and process until smooth. Heat pesto in a large skillet over medium-low heat. Add cream, wine, salt, and pepper. Simmer for 5 minutes. Add tomatoes and toss lightly. Drain sun dried tomatoes and chop coarsely. Add to pesto cream and toss lightly to heat through. Serve over Pasta Fresca and crusty sourdough bread.

Preparation Time: 40 minutes (includes soaking time)
Cooking Time: 10 to 15 minutes
Serves: 4

Pasta Fresca

2 cups semolina flour or all-purpose flour

3 eggs, slightly beaten

2 tablespoons olive oil

Water

Place flour in a food processor. Add beaten eggs, 1 tablespoon oil, and ½ teaspoon water with motor running. Process mixture until it begins to form a ball, about 15 seconds.

Place the dough onto a lightly floured board and knead for 3 to 5 minutes until smooth (do not overknead, or dough will become tough). Allow dough to stand for 30 minutes, covered with a damp cloth. Process small amounts of dough through a pasta machine, using manufacturer's instructions.

Bring 6 to 8 quarts salted water to a boil. Add 1 tablespoon olive oil. Add fresh pasta and continue to boil for 3 to 4 minutes (do not overcook, pasta should be tender, yet firm). Drain, but do not rinse.

Preparation Time: 35 minutes

Cooking Time: 3 to 5 minutes

Makes: 1 pound of pasta

Note: 1½ cups semolina or all-purpose flour and ½ cup whole wheat flour may be used for a uniquely nutty flavor.

Spinach Enchiladas

2 packages frozen chopped spinach,
   pressed dry
1 envelope dry onion soup mix
¾ pound shredded sharp Cheddar
   cheese

¾ pound shredded Monterey jack
   cheese
12 flour tortillas
½ pint heavy cream

Preheat oven to 350 degrees.

Combine spinach and onion soup mix. Blend in half of the Cheddar and jack cheeses. Save remaining cheeses for topping. Place about 2 heaping tablespoons of the spinach mixture down the middle of a tortilla and roll. Place seam side down in a 9 × 13-inch baking dish. Repeat with remaining tortillas. Pour cream over enchiladas and sprinkle with remaining cheeses. Bake covered for 20 minutes. Uncover and bake for 15 minutes longer.

Preparation Time: 30 minutes

Cooking Time: 35 minutes

Serves: 6 to 8

Note: Freezes well. May be made ahead and frozen before the cream and remaining cheeses are added. Thaw in the refrigerator the night before cooking.

Vegetable Frittata

3 tablespoons oil
¾ cup chopped onion
2 large cloves garlic, minced
½ cup chopped green bell pepper
½ cup chopped red bell pepper
2 cups sliced mushrooms
2 cups chopped zucchini
6 eggs
¼ cup light cream

1½ cups shredded Cheddar cheese
8 ounces cream cheese, diced into
     ½-inch cubes
1 teaspoon salt
½ teaspoon pepper
2 teaspoons Worcestershire sauce
1 cup seasoned bread crumbs

Preheat oven to 350 degrees.

Heat oil in a large skillet. Sauté onion and garlic until transparent. Add vegetables and sauté until tender. Remove from heat and set aside to cool. Beat eggs and cream. Add cheeses, salt, pepper, Worcestershire sauce, bread crumbs, and cooled vegetables and mix. Pour into a lightly oiled 9-inch springform pan. Bake for 1 hour or until set in center and golden.

Preparation Time: 30 minutes
Cooking Time: 1 hour
Serves: 6 to 8

Note: The delicate blend of fresh vegetables, eggs, and cheese offers an elegant brunch or late supper.

Almond Dill Torte

1 cup whole wheat bread crumbs
1 cup ground almonds
½ cup butter, softened
12 ounces cream cheese, softened
1 cup ricotta cheese
2 eggs

⅓ cup fresh dill
4 tablespoons light cream
1 tablespoon grated lemon rind
1 teaspoon nutmeg
Salt
Fresh dill sprigs for garnish

Preheat oven to 350 degrees.

Combine bread crumbs, almonds, and butter. Oil a 9-inch springform pan. Pat mixture onto the bottom and up the sides of the pan. Blend cheeses, eggs, dill, cream, lemon rind, nutmeg, and salt in a food processor until mixture is smooth. Pour into crust and bake for 45 minutes. Cool and transfer torte to a serving platter. Garnish with sprigs of dill.

Preparation Time: 30 minutes
Cooking Time: 45 minutes
Serves: 8

Celery Seed Dip

¼ cup sugar
1 teaspoon flour
1 egg yolk
2 tablespoons lemon juice
½ cup pineapple juice

1 tablespoon celery seed
1 cup heavy cream, whipped
Assorted fresh fruits for dipping

Combine sugar, flour, and egg yolk in a small saucepan. Add fruit juices and simmer over low heat until thick, stirring constantly for about 10 minutes. Add celery seed. Chill in refrigerator. Fold in whipped cream. Serve with fresh fruit.

Preparation Time: 20 minutes
Cooking Time: 10 minutes
Makes: Approximately 2 cups

Apple Cheese Torte

Crust
½ cup butter

⅓ cup sugar

¼ teaspoon vanilla

1 cup flour

Combine ingredients and press onto the bottom and up the sides of an oiled 9-inch springform pan. Set aside.

Filling
8 ounces cream cheese, softened

1 egg

½ teaspoon vanilla

¼ cup sugar

Preheat oven to 450 degrees.

Blend ingredients together. Beat until fluffy. Spread over crust. Bake for 10 minutes.

Topping
⅓ cup sugar

1 teaspoon cinnamon

4 cups thinly sliced Granny Smith apples

¼ cup coarsely ground almonds

Toss together sugar, cinnamon, and apples gently to coat. Layer apples over the filling. Sprinkle almonds on top. Lower oven temperature and bake at 400 degrees for 25 minutes.

Preparation Time: 1 hour

Cooking Time: 35 minutes

Serves: 8 to 10

Easy Pan Popover Puff

1 cup milk
⅔ cup flour
2 tablespoons sugar
½ teaspoon salt
2 eggs
½ teaspoon grated lemon peel
½ teaspoon cardamon

¼ cup butter
Whipping cream to serve
Fresh strawberries to serve
Sour cream to serve
Cinnamon-sugar to serve
Preserves or jam to serve

Preheat oven to 400 degrees.

Combine all ingredients except butter in a blender and blend until smooth. Melt butter in a 9-inch pie plate in the oven. Remove from oven and pour batter into pie plate. Bake for 35 minutes until golden and puffy (it should be moist in the center). Serve immediately with toppings of your choice.

Preparation Time: 10 minutes

Cooking Time: 35 minutes

Serves: 4

Brunch Eggs California

2 cups fresh corn, approximately 2 ears
2 tablespoons butter
12 eggs
1½ cups sour cream
½ cup milk
4 cups shredded Cheddar cheese
8 ounces diced green chiles

1 tablespoon Worcestershire sauce
1 tablespoon salt
1 teaspoon pepper
Sour cream to serve
Chopped tomatoes to serve
Guacamole to serve (recipe page 40)
Salsa Fresca to serve (recipe page 147)

Preheat oven to 325 degrees.

Sauté corn in butter for 5 minutes or until just tender. Set aside to cool. Beat eggs. Add remaining ingredients and mix well. Add cooled corn and mix. Pour into an oiled 9 × 13-inch baking dish and bake for 1 hour 15 minutes or until firm and golden on top. Serve with sour cream, tomatoes, Guacamole, and Salsa Fresca.

Preparation Time: 20 minutes

Cooking Time: 1 hour 15 minutes

Serves: 8 to 10

Huevos Monterey

Salsa Fresca

2 ripe tomatoes	2 teaspoons juice of pickled peppers
½ onion	½ cup chopped fresh cilantro
½ cup chopped green bell pepper	Salt
3 cloves garlic	1½ cups tomato juice
4 pickled hot chile peppers	

Combine tomatoes and onion in a food processor. Pulse until coarsely chopped. Add bell pepper, garlic, pickled peppers, and juice of peppers. Pulse 2 or 3 times. Add cilantro, salt, and tomato juice. Pulse until well blended but chunky. Store in an airtight container. Will keep for several days. Best if made 1 day in advance.

Tortilla Cups
8 flour tortillas
Oil

Preheat oven to 325 degrees.

Rub flour tortillas with oil on both sides. Place tortillas down gently into small Pyrex cups, making soft folds in the sides of the tortilla in order to form the cup. Bake for 15 minutes or until golden and crispy. Allow to cool before removing tortilla cups.

Eggs

1 recipe Salsa Fresca (recipe above)	2½ cups Black Beans with Chorizo (recipe page 239) or refried beans, heated
8 eggs	1 cup shredded Monterey jack cheese
8 tortilla cups (recipe above)	Cilantro sprigs for garnish

Bring salsa to a boil in a large skillet. Reduce to a strong simmer. Drop eggs into the hot salsa gently and cover. Poach the eggs.

Place 1 tablespoon of the beans on each plate. Set the tortilla cups on the beans to keep the cups stationary. Place ¼ cup beans in each cup. Top beans with poached egg and salsa (be careful not to break the egg). Top each egg with jack cheese and cilantro sprig.

Preparation Time: 30 to 40 minutes (not including preparation of the Black Beans with Chorizo)

Cooking Time: Approximately 25 minutes (includes baking the Tortilla cups)

Serves: 8

Sicilian Eggs on Polenta

Polenta is a cornmeal porridge served in place of bread. It may be thick and porridge-like or molded and sliced. It is frequently served with cheese and a tomato sauce.

Polenta

1 teaspoon salt
4½ cups water
2 cups medium-grain yellow cornmeal

1 tablespoon butter
2 cloves garlic, minced

Bring salted water to a boil in a saucepan. Lower heat to a simmer and slowly add cornmeal, stirring continuously with a wire whisk to avoid lumps. Continue stirring with a wooden spoon after all the meal has been added (the meal will thicken gradually and pop with bubbles). Add butter and garlic. Cook the polenta for 20 to 30 minutes, stirring constantly (should be a soft porridge with no bite or raw taste). Spoon onto a bread board and shape into a loaf or pour into a loaf pan. Allow it to cool and become firm. Slice into ½-inch thick slices. Cover with a damp cloth and set aside.

Sauce Sicilian

2 tablespoons olive oil
½ onion, chopped
1 large clove garlic, minced
⅓ cup chopped green bell pepper
⅓ cup chopped red bell pepper
⅓ cup chopped yellow bell pepper
2 cups tomato sauce
1 cup water

½ teaspoon dried basil leaves
½ teaspoon dried oregano leaves
½ teaspoon fennel seed
Salt
Pepper
Dash cayenne pepper
2 teaspoons sugar

Heat oil in a large skillet. Sauté onion and garlic until tender. Add bell peppers and sauté until tender. Add remaining ingredients. Simmer for 15 to 30 minutes. May be refrigerated at this point. Refrigerating overnight will enhance the flavor. Makes approximately 4½ cups.

Eggs

4½ cups Sauce Sicilian (recipe above)
2 tablespoons olive oil
Polenta, sliced (recipe above)

6 to 8 eggs
1 cup freshly grated Parmesan cheese

Bring Sauce Sicilian to a strong simmer. Heat 2 tablespoons olive oil and fry sliced polenta until browned in another skillet. Fry as many pieces as needed for serving. Set aside.

Continued on next page

Drop eggs into simmering sauce and poach. Place fried polenta onto each plate, 1 or 2 pieces per serving. Spoon eggs onto fried polenta and cover with sauce. Top with Parmesan cheese and serve.

Preparation Time: 30 minutes

Cooking Time: 45 minutes to 1 hour (includes polenta, sauce, and eggs)

Serves: 6 to 8

Mushroom Crust Crab Quiche

5 tablespoons butter
½ pound mushrooms, finely chopped
½ cup crushed crackers (about 16)
1¼ teaspoons dried tarragon leaves
¾ cup chopped green onions
¾ cup shredded Monterey jack
    cheese

¾ cup shredded Swiss cheese
6 ounces crab
¾ cup small curd cottage cheese
¼ cup ricotta cheese
3 eggs
¼ teaspoon cayenne pepper
2 tablespoons sherry

Preheat oven to 350 degrees.

Melt 3 tablespoons butter in a skillet. Add mushrooms and sauté until tender. Remove from heat. Stir in crushed crackers and 1 teaspoon tarragon. Press into an oiled 9-inch pie plate. Bake for 15 minutes.

Melt remaining butter. Add onions and sauté until tender. Spread onions over cooked mushroom crust. Blend remaining ¼ teaspoon tarragon and remaining ingredients together. Pour over onions. Bake for about 40 minutes or until firm. Allow to sit for 5 minutes before serving.

Preparation Time: 30 minutes

Cooking Time: 55 minutes

Serves: 4 to 6

Cornbread Soufflé

4 cups milk
1 cup cornmeal
¾ teaspoon salt
2 teaspoons baking powder
2 teaspoons sugar

2 tablespoons butter
6 eggs, separated
Sour cream to serve
Strawberry jam to serve

Preheat oven to 400 degrees.

Heat 2 cups milk to boiling while soaking the cornmeal in the remaining 2 cups milk. Add cornmeal mixture to hot milk and cook until thick and soft, but not dry. Remove from heat and add remaining dry ingredients and butter. Beat until cooled. Add egg yolks 1 at a time, beating well after each addition. Beat egg whites until stiff peaks form. Fold beaten egg whites into the cornmeal mixture. Bake in 2 oiled 2-quart soufflé dishes for 30 minutes. Serve immediately with sour cream and strawberry jam.

Preparation Time: 15 minutes
Cooking Time: 30 minutes
Serves: 5 to 6

Eggs Mornay

½ cup plus 2 tablespoons butter
1 teaspoon salt
¼ teaspoon pepper
½ cup flour
3 cups milk, scalded
1 cup diced Swiss cheese
¾ cup grated Parmesan cheese

3 tablespoons sherry
12 eggs, hard boiled and peeled
½ pound mushrooms, minced
¼ cup chopped fresh parsley
1 teaspoon dried tarragon leaves
Dash cayenne pepper
½ cup seasoned bread crumbs

Combine 4 tablespoons softened butter, salt, pepper, flour, and 2 cups scalded milk in a blender. Blend well. Pour into a saucepan and add remaining scalded milk. Cook over medium heat, stirring constantly until sauce thickens and bubbles. Add Swiss cheese, ½ cup Parmesan cheese, and sherry. Stir until cheese is melted. Remove from heat and cover.

Cut eggs in half lengthwise. Empty yolks into a bowl. Set aside. Melt 4 tablespoons butter in a skillet. Sauté mushrooms. Stir in parsley, tarragon, and cayenne pepper. Mash the yolks with ½ cup of the sauce. Add mushrooms to yolk mixture and mix.

Preheat oven to 350 degrees.

Fill egg whites with mushroom mixture. Spread a thin layer of sauce in a shallow baking dish and arrange eggs on the sauce. Spoon remaining sauce over all. Toss bread crumbs and the remaining ¼ cup Parmesan cheese with 2 tablespoons melted butter. Sprinkle over the eggs. Bake for 30 minutes.

Preparation Time: 45 minutes
Cooking Time: 30 minutes
Serves: 6 to 8

Note: This may also be made into individual servings using ramekins or other individual serving dishes.

Seafood

Broiled Salmon with Beurre Blanc Sauce

Chervil is frequently referred to as the "gourmet's" parsley. It enhances other herbs and is sweeter and more aromatic than parsley.

Wine Suggestion: Chardonnay or Sauvignon Blanc

4 salmon steaks, 1-inch thick
½ cup dry white wine
2 teaspoons white wine vinegar
¾ teaspoon minced fresh tarragon or
    ¼ teaspoon dried
¼ teaspoon dried chervil

⅛ teaspoon white pepper
2 shallots, sliced
½ cup butter
2 tablespoons heavy cream
4 teaspoons chopped fresh tarragon
    for garnish

Preheat broiler.

Lightly oil broiler pan and broil steaks for 4 to 5 minutes on each side. Remove from oven and keep warm.

Bring wine, vinegar, tarragon, chervil, pepper, and shallots to a boil over medium-high heat. Boil for 5 minutes or until liquid is reduced to 2 tablespoons. Remove shallots and discard. Reduce heat to medium and add butter, beating with a wire whisk until slightly thickened. Remove from heat and stir in cream. Spoon sauce over steaks and serve. Garnish each steak with 1 teaspoon fresh tarragon.

Preparation Time: 20 minutes
Cooking Time: 10 minutes
Serves: 4

Note: Salmon may also be barbequed for approximately 5 minutes per side.

Poached Salmon in Mustard Sauce

Wine Suggestion:
Chardonnay or
Sauvignon Blanc

Poached Salmon

1 onion, coarsely chopped

¼ cup coarsely chopped celery

1 cup dry white wine

2 cups water

4 6-ounce salmon fillets

Combine onion, celery, wine, and water in a skillet. Heat to a simmer and add salmon. Poach for 4 minutes, covered, until salmon feels firm yet springy.

Mustard Sauce

½ cup sour cream

½ cup yogurt

1 tablespoon Dijon mustard

3 dashes Tabasco sauce

2 teaspoons fresh dill

¼ teaspoon fresh dill

¼ teaspoon salt (optional)

Caviar for garnish

Fresh dill for garnish

Combine all ingredients. Arrange salmon on plates and spoon sauce over fish. Garnish with caviar and dill.

Preparation Time: 15 minutes

Cooking Time: 4 minutes

Serves: 4

Maine Lobster Tacos

This recipe is from the popular California Mexican restaurant Rebecca's.

For Each Person
2 pink grapefruit
1 fresh serrano chile
⅛ medium purple onion
2 tablespoons coarsely chopped fresh cilantro

½ teaspoon salt
1 1½-pound Maine lobster
Fresh tortillas to serve

Salsa

Remove the sections of grapefruit with a sharp knife. Cut sections into ¼-inch lengths and dice. Cut the serrano chile in half lengthwise and slice into thin half moons. Dice the purple onion finely (⅛-inch). Combine the grapefruit, chile, onion, and cilantro. Add salt. Drain in a colander. Set aside.

Lobsters

Cut live lobsters in half lengthwise. Rinse the body cavities and disjoin claws at the body. Crack the claws with the back of a heavy knife until the shell is well broken. Broil the lobsters and claws in a hot oven, or better yet, char them, meat side first, on an outdoor barbeque. Arrange the lobsters, meat side up, on the serving platter and fill the cavities with the grapefruit salsa. Arrange the claws around the lobsters. Serve with warm tortillas.

Preparation Time: 20 minutes each
Cooking Time: Approximately 10 minutes

Lobster Dijonnaise

Wine Suggestion:
Chardonnay

Photograph featured
on Dust Jacket.

6 lobster tails, halved, cooked, and chilled

6 tablespoons mayonnaise

1 teaspoon Dijon mustard

1 teaspoon fresh lemon juice

1 teaspoon tarragon wine vinegar

1 tablespoon finely minced fresh chives

1 tablespoon finely minced fresh parsley

Salt

Pepper

Bibb or red leaf lettuce leaves for garnish

Capers for garnish

Remove lobster meat from tails. Reserve shells for serving. Chop meat into small pieces and set aside. Combine remaining ingredients and blend well. Add lobster. Toss with a fork and refrigerate until chilled. Stuff shells with lobster mixture and place on lettuce lined plates to serve. Garnish with capers.

Preparation Time: 20 minutes

Serves: 6

Grilled Tuna Santa Fe

½ cup fresh lime juice

½ cup beer

3 tablespoons oil

4 teaspoons cumin

4 teaspoons Dijon mustard

½ teaspoon salt

4 cloves garlic, minced

4 to 6 yellowfin or albacore tuna fillets

Salsa Fresca to serve (recipe page 147)

Sliced avocado to serve

Combine lime juice, beer, oil, cumin, mustard, salt, and garlic in a large shallow dish. Marinate fillets for 2 hours, turning occasionally.

Preheat grill.

Grill fillets for 5 minutes on each side. Serve with Salsa Fresca and sliced avocado.

Preparation Time: 2 hours 10 minutes

Cooking Time: 10 minutes

Serves: 4 to 6

Grilled Ceviche

A member of the
Junior League of Los
Angeles won
national recognition
for this recipe in a
cooking contest
judged by the late
James Beard.

1 pound fresh red snapper
½ cup olive oil
Juice of 2 limes
2 tomatoes, chopped
½ cup chopped fresh cilantro

½ onion, chopped
Salt
Pepper
1 cup Salsa Fresca (recipe page 147)

Rinse snapper and place in a shallow dish. Combine oil and lime juice. Pour lime mixture over snapper, turning twice, and then cover. Marinate for 15 minutes, turn, cover, and marinate for 15 minutes more (flesh will appear gray because the lime juice is "cooking" the fish, just like in a true ceviche).

Preheat grill.

Combine tomatoes, cilantro, onion, salt, and pepper. Add to the Salsa Fresca and mix well. Cover fish with salsa. Grill fish for 3 minutes on each side, basting well. Serve with remaining salsa.

Preparation Time: 45 minutes
Cooking Time: 6 minutes
Serves: 2

Red Snapper in Mustard Cream

1 tablespoon butter
¼ cup finely chopped green onions
3 tablespoons white wine
¾ cup heavy cream
1 pound fresh red snapper fillets

1 tablespoon Dijon mustard
1 firm ripe tomato, peeled, seeded,
   and chopped
8 chives, cut into 2-inch pieces

Melt butter in a large skillet over medium-low heat. Add onions and stir for 3 minutes or until tender. Stir in wine and boil until most of the liquid has evaporated, about 1 minute. Add cream and simmer for approximately 1 minute, until thickened. Cut fillets in half to provide 4 serving portions if fillets are too large. Place snapper in sauce and poach covered for 3 to 4 minutes. Remove snapper carefully to a warm dish and cover. Whisk mustard into sauce over low heat (do not let it boil). Spoon approximately ¼ of the mustard sauce onto each of 4 plates, covering an area slightly larger than the fish portions. Place the snapper on top of the mustard sauce and top with tomato. Garnish with 2 pieces of chives crossed.

Preparation Time: 15 minutes
Cooking Time: 5 to 6 minutes
Serves: 4

Seafood Baja

Wine Suggestion:
Chenin Blanc

3 tablespoons butter

3 tablespoons oil

3 cloves garlic, minced

½ red bell pepper, chunked

½ green bell pepper, chunked

6 green onions, chopped

¾ pound halibut or white fish, chunked

½ pound medium raw shrimp, shelled and deveined

1 cup green seedless grapes

¼ cup lime juice

1 tablespoon chopped fresh cilantro or 1 teaspoon ground coriander

Rice to serve

Lemon or lime slices for garnish

Cilantro sprigs for garnish

Heat butter and oil in a large skillet. Add garlic, bell peppers, onions, and seafood. Sauté, stirring constantly until fish flakes easily and shrimp turns pink. Add grapes, lime juice, and cilantro. Turn off heat. Allow skillet to sit for 5 minutes on burner. Serve over rice. Garnish with citrus slices and cilantro sprigs.

Preparation Time: 15 minutes

Cooking Time: 10 to 15 minutes

Serves: 2 to 4

Note: Cooked shrimp may be substituted for raw shrimp. Add when grapes are added. This dish is an intriguing combination of flavors.

Seafood Baja.

Lemon Soy Swordfish Steaks with Avocado Butter

Lemon Soy Swordfish Steaks

⅔ cup soy sauce

2 teaspoons grated lemon peel

½ cup fresh lemon juice

5 cloves garlic, minced

4 teaspoons Dijon mustard

1 cup olive oil or ½ cup olive oil and ½ cup safflower oil

8 small swordfish steaks

Avocado Butter (recipe below)

Blend soy sauce, lemon peel, lemon juice, garlic, and mustard in a blender. Add oil slowly in a thin stream until well blended. Place swordfish in a shallow baking dish. Pour marinade over fish. Prick fish with a fork and turn occasionally. Allow to marinate for 1 to 3 hours, covered in the refrigerator.

Preheat grill.

Grill over hot coals for 5 to 6 minutes per side. Brush steaks frequently with marinade. Top with Avocado Butter and serve.

Avocado Butter

½ cup butter, softened

½ cup ripe avocado

5 tablespoons chopped fresh parsley

2 cloves garlic, minced

Juice of 1 small lime

Salt

Whip butter in a small mixing bowl until soft and creamy. Blend in avocado, parsley, and garlic. Beat in lime juice and salt. Refrigerate until needed. Serve at room temperature.

Preparation Time: 15 minutes plus 1 to 3 hours marinating time for fish, 15 minutes for Avocado Butter

Cooking Time: 10 to 12 minutes

Serves: 8

Note: Marinade is also excellent with halibut and shark.

Grilled Swordfish with
Green Peppercorn Sauce

*Arrowroot is the
starch of a tropical
plant used as a
thickener for soups
and sauces. It does
not cloud up like
flour as it thickens
so it is best used in
soups, sauces,
gravies, and glazes
that must be clear.*

*Wine Suggestion:
Pinot Noir or
Chardonnay*

1 tablespoon olive oil
2 shallots, minced
2 tablespoons Cognac
4 swordfish steaks
½ cup heavy cream

½ cup beef broth
1 tablespoon lightly crushed green peppercorns
½ teaspoon arrowroot

Oil and preheat grill.

Heat olive oil in a small skillet. Add shallots and sauté until golden. Add Cognac and simmer for 1 to 2 minutes. Set aside. Place swordfish steaks on grill. Grill for 6 to 8 minutes per side, depending on thickness. Add cream and broth to shallot and Cognac mixture. Bring to a boil. Add peppercorns. Reduce heat and simmer for 2 to 3 minutes. Sprinkle arrowroot over mixture, stirring until blended, and heat for an additional 2 minutes or until thickened. Pour sauce over steaks.

Preparation Time: 10 minutes

Cooking Time: 15 minutes

Serves: 4

Note: Shark or tuna fillets may be substituted for the swordfish. The peppercorn sauce is also excellent served over grilled sliced steak.

Poached Fillet of Sole

Wine Suggestion:
Chardonnay,
Sauvignon Blanc, or
Semillon

1 cup minced mushrooms
1 cup minced fresh parsley
¼ cup minced shallots
Salt
¼ teaspoon white pepper

2 tablespoons butter
1½ pounds fillet of sole
1 cup white wine
1 cup clam juice

Preheat oven to 350 degrees.

Toss mushrooms, parsley, and shallots with salt and pepper. Butter a 9 × 13-inch stove-to-oven baking dish. Spread mushroom mixture over bottom of dish. Spread fillets out flat, covering mushroom mixture. Pour wine and clam juice over fillets. Place on top of stove and simmer. Transfer to oven for 10 minutes. Serve fish with mushrooms, parsley, and shallots mixture spooned over the top.

Preparation Time: 30 minutes

Cooking Time: 10 minutes

Serves: 4

Sole with Creamy Wine Sauce

Wine Suggestion:
Chardonnay or
Sauvignon Blanc

4 8-ounce sole fillets
Salt
White pepper
2 tablespoons chopped green onions
2 teaspoons chopped fresh Italian parsley
¼ teaspoon White Wine Worcestershire sauce
½ teaspoon finely grated lemon peel

½ cup dry white wine
1 tablespoon freshly squeezed lemon juice
½ cup Crème Fraîche (recipe page 138) or heavy cream
1 teaspoon arrowroot
1 cup seedless red grapes
1 tablespoon finely chopped hazelnuts

Rinse fillets in cold water and pat dry. Season lightly with salt and pepper. Roll fillets and arrange in a medium skillet. Combine green onions, parsley, White Wine Worcestershire sauce, lemon peel, wine, and lemon juice. Pour over fillets, cover, and bring to a quick boil. Lower heat and simmer for 5 minutes. Remove to a warm baking dish. Reduce liquid to ½ cup by boiling. Add Crème Fraîche and arrowroot stirring constantly, until slightly thickened.

Preheat broiler.

Pour sauce over fillets. Add grapes and sprinkle with hazelnuts. Broil for 1 minute or until sauce bubbles. Spoon sauce over fish and serve immediately.

Preparation Time: 15 minutes
Cooking Time: 10 minutes
Serves: 4

Baked Halibut with Italian Olive Tomato Sauce

Wine Suggestion:
Zinfandel

2 tablespoons olive oil

4 cloves garlic, minced

1 white onion, diced

¼ cup tomato paste

3 tablespoons flour

1 tablespoon chopped fresh oregano

1 tablespoon chopped fresh basil

1 teaspoon chopped fresh thyme

½ teaspoon chopped fresh rosemary

1 tablespoon chopped fresh parsley

1 bay leaf

10 ripe tomatoes, puréed

¼ cup dry Italian olives, chopped

Salt

Pepper

4 halibut steaks, brushed with olive oil

Sprigs of fresh herbs

Whole Italian olives for garnish

Heat olive oil in a large saucepan. Add garlic and onion and sauté slowly for 2 minutes. Stir in tomato paste and cook, stirring for 1 minute. Add flour and herbs and blend well. Pour in tomato purée. Bring to a boil. Lower heat and simmer for 30 minutes, stirring often. Force sauce through a coarse sieve. Discard the herb and onion residue. Add olives, salt, and pepper.

Preheat oven to 350 degrees.

Place halibut on an oiled baking sheet. Season with salt and pepper. Bake for 15 minutes. Serve sauce over halibut or place halibut in a pool of the sauce. Garnish with additional sprigs of fresh herbs and whole dry Italian olives.

Preparation Time: 15 minutes

Cooking Time: 35 minutes

Serves: 4

Baked Halibut with Italian Olive Tomato Sauce.

Halibut with California Butters

Wine Suggestion:
Chardonnay or
Sauvignon Blanc

Halibut

1 pound fresh halibut, fillets or steaks   **Citrus Chili Butter (recipe below)**
Pistachio Orange Butter (recipe below)   **Walnut Thyme Butter (recipe below)**

Lightly oil and preheat grill. Grill halibut approximately 5-inches from flame for about 5 minutes. Turn halibut and continue cooking until halibut has lost its translucency. Remove halibut to a serving dish or individual plates. Serve with assorted sliced butters.

Preparation Time: 5 minutes

Cooking Time: 10 minutes

Serves: 4

Note: Broil halibut 6-inches from heat source for about 5 minutes per side for an indoor alternative.

Pistachio Orange Butter
½ cup butter, softened   **1½ teaspoons orange juice**
2½ tablespoons chopped pistachios   **½ teaspoon minced garlic**
1 tablespoon minced fresh parsley

Citrus Chili Butter
½ cup butter, softened   **1 teaspoon grated lemon zest**
1 teaspoon grated orange zest   **1 teaspoon chili powder**
1 teaspoon grated lime zest   **½ teaspoon cayenne pepper**

Walnut Thyme Butter
½ cup butter, softened   **1½ teaspoons fresh lime juice**
2 tablespoons finely chopped walnuts   **½ teaspoon coarse grind pepper**
1 tablespoon crushed fresh thyme

The Following Instructions Are For Each Butter Recipe.

Whip the butter. Add the remaining ingredients and mix thoroughly. Place seasoned butter onto a sheet of plastic wrap. Fold plastic wrap around butter and roll into a 1-inch thick log. Tightly twist ends of plastic wrap and refrigerate until firm, at least 30 minutes. Slice butter for serving.

Preparation Time: 10 minutes

Makes: Approximately ½ cup per seasoned butter

Orange Roughy Fillets with Yogurt Glaze

2 pounds orange roughy fillets
Salt
White pepper
½ cup nonfat plain yogurt
2 tablespoons prepared horseradish
4 teaspoons dry mustard
¼ cup freshly grated Parmesan cheese

2 tablespoons freshly squeezed lemon juice
3 tablespoons chopped fresh dill or 1½ teaspoons dried
2 tablespoons capers
Lemon slices for garnish

Rinse fillets in cold water and pat dry. Season with salt and pepper. Place in a large glass baking dish.

Preheat oven to 350 degrees.

Combine yogurt, horseradish, mustard, Parmesan cheese, and lemon juice. Baste both sides of fish with a thin layer of yogurt sauce. Sprinkle with dill and capers. Bake for 10 to 12 minutes or to desired doneness. Garnish with lemon slices.

Preparation Time: 15

Cooking Time: 10 to 12 minutes

Serves: 4

Note: Sole or red snapper fillets may be substituted.

Grilled Shark Teriyaki

Wine Suggestion:
Pinot Noir or
Chardonnay

½ **cup soy sauce**
¼ **cup water**
¼ **cup pale dry sherry**
2 **cloves garlic, finely chopped**

1 **tablespoon sugar**
2 **teaspoons minced fresh ginger**
4 **shark fillets**

Combine all ingredients except shark fillets. Mix well. Pour over fillets, turning to coat each side. Refrigerate and marinate for 1 to 2 hours, turning occasionally.

Oil and preheat grill. Grill fillets for 5 to 6 minutes per side.

Preparation Time: 10 minutes

Cooking Time: 10 to 15 minutes

Serves: 4

Note: Swordfish may be substituted for shark.

Baked Sand Dabs with Grapefruit and Ginger

1 **pound sand dab fillets**
2 **tablespoons butter**
1 **pink grapefruit, sectioned and juice reserved**

1 **tablespoon soy sauce**
½ **teaspoon grated fresh ginger**
1 **tablespoon chopped fresh parsley**
Pink grapefruit sections for garnish

Preheat oven to 350 degrees.

Arrange fish in a shallow baking dish and dot with butter. Combine grapefruit sections and juice, soy sauce, ginger, and parsley. Pour over fish. Bake until fish is opaque, about 10 to 15 minutes. Garnish with grapefruit sections.

Preparation Time: 10 minutes

Cooking Time: 15 minutes

Serves: 2

Red Pepper Scallops and Pasta

12 ounces spinach fettucini

4 tablespoons butter

¼ cup olive oil

3 red bell peppers, slivered

2 cloves garlic, minced

½ teaspoon dried red pepper flakes

¾ cup chicken broth

¼ cup fresh lemon juice

1 pound medium scallops

1 cup sliced mushrooms

¾ cup chopped fresh parsley

Zest of 1 lemon

Salt

Pepper

Cook the fettucini according to package directions and drain. Set aside.

Heat butter and oil in a skillet over medium-high heat. Add bell peppers, garlic, and red pepper flakes. Sauté for 1 minute. Remove bell peppers and set aside. Add broth and lemon juice to skillet. Bring to a boil. Add scallops and mushrooms. Cover and simmer for about 5 minutes, until scallops are opaque. Remove from heat. Remove scallops from skillet and set aside. Toss fettucini with mushrooms and broth in skillet to warm. Place on a serving dish. Top with bell peppers, scallops, parsley, and lemon zest. Season with salt and pepper.

Preparation Time: 20 minutes

Cooking Time: 15 to 20 minutes

Serves: 4 to 6

Linguini with Shrimp and Sun Dried Tomatoes in Mustard Sauce

Wine Suggestion:
Chardonnay or
Sauvignon Blanc

2 tablespoons unsalted butter
2 tablespoons olive oil
1 medium onion, chopped
4 large cloves garlic, minced
½ cup sun dried tomatoes packed in oil, drained and cut into thin strips
¼ cup minced fresh parsley
2 tablespoons capers
½ cup dry white wine

12 jumbo shrimp, shelled and deveined
2 tablespoons Dijon mustard
½ cup heavy cream
½ teaspoon salt
½ teaspoon freshly ground pepper
1 pound linguini
Fresh tarragon sprigs for garnish

Heat butter and oil in a large heavy skillet. Add onion, garlic, sun dried tomatoes, parsley, and capers. Sauté over moderate heat until onion is tender but not brown. Add wine and allow to simmer for 2 minutes. Add shrimp and continue cooking until the shrimp turn pink and are no longer transparent, about 2 minutes. Add mustard and cream and stir until sauce thickens, about 2 minutes. Season with salt and pepper. Cook linguini according to package directions. Serve shrimp mixture over linguini and garnish with fresh tarragon sprigs.

Preparation Time: 25 minutes
Cooking Time: 15 minutes
Serves: 2

Shrimp in Puff Pastry

3 tablespoons butter

4 artichoke hearts packed in water, drained and quartered

8 ounces sliced fresh mushrooms

1 tablespoon dried parsley flakes

1 tablespoon garlic salt

1 10 × 15-inch sheet puff pastry (fresh or frozen)

10 ounces Swiss cheese, sliced

12 jumbo shrimp, cooked, shelled, and deveined

2 tablespoons grated Parmesan cheese

1 egg, beaten

½ teaspoon minced fresh parsley

Melt butter in a large skillet over medium-high heat. Add artichoke hearts, mushrooms, parsley flakes, and garlic salt. Sauté until mushrooms are tender. Allow mixture to cool. Drain well. Set aside.

Oil a large rimmed baking sheet. Place puff pastry on baking sheet. Overlap Swiss cheese slices lengthwise along right half of pastry leaving a 1-inch border at the long edge and ½-inch border at each end. Arrange artichoke hearts over cheese, spreading evenly. Spoon mushrooms over cheese and artichoke hearts. Arrange rows of shrimp on top of mushrooms. Sprinkle 1 tablespoon of Parmesan cheese on top. Brush borders with half of the beaten egg. Fold left half of dough over filling, pressing edges firmly with fork to seal (may be prepared up to 8 hours ahead at this point, covered with foil or plastic wrap, and refrigerated).

Preheat oven to 475 degrees.

Brush pastry with remaining egg. Sprinkle with parsley and remaining Parmesan cheese. Bake for 15 minutes. Reduce oven temperature to 375 degrees and bake until golden, about 15 to 20 minutes.

Preparation Time: 30 minutes

Cooking Time: 35 minutes

Serves: 4 to 6

Malay Shrimp Satay

2 tablespoons sliced green onions
2 cloves garlic, minced
2 tablespoons oil
¾ cup chicken broth
3 tablespoons peanut butter
1 tablespoon soy sauce
½ teaspoon finely grated lemon peel
¼ teaspoon cayenne pepper

1 tablespoon lemon juice
1 teaspoon chili powder
½ teaspoon brown sugar
¼ teaspoon ground ginger
1 pound jumbo shrimp, shelled, deveined, and with tails intact
Rice to serve
Finely chopped peanuts for garnish

Sauté onions and garlic in oil until tender but not brown. Add remaining ingredients except shrimp. Simmer sauce uncovered for 10 minutes, stirring frequently. Remove from heat and cool. Marinate shrimp in cooled peanut mixture for 1 hour, turning often to coat well. Remove shrimp, reserving peanut sauce.

Preheat grill or broiler.

Thread shrimp onto bamboo skewers in serpentine fashion. Grill or broil until shrimp turns pink or to desired doneness. Serve over rice. Sprinkle chopped peanuts over skewered shrimp and serve with peanut sauce for dipping.

Preparation Time: 40 minutes
Cooking Time: 5 minutes
Serves: 4

Note: Very spicy.

Malay Shrimp
Satay.

California Shrimp Toss

Water
2 tablespoons salt
4 lemons
8 whole onions
1 package crab boil
¼ cup Tabasco sauce (season to
    desired spiciness)

8 to 10 whole red potatoes
4 to 6 ears of corn
4 pounds jumbo shrimp
Butter to serve

Fill a large pot with water and bring to a boil. Add salt. Cut lemons in half, squeeze juice into pot, and then drop remaining lemon in, peel and all. Add onions, crab boil, Tabasco sauce, and potatoes and cover. Boil for about 40 minutes or until potatoes float. Add corn and cook for 10 minutes. Add shrimp and cook for 3 to 5 minutes longer. Serve with warm butter for corn and potatoes.

Preparation Time: 10 minutes

Cooking Time: Approximately 1 hour

Serves: 8

Note: This recipe is meant to be served in a very dramatic way. Cover the table with newspaper, then put freezer paper down the center. Drain the pot completely and remove the crab boil bag. After the guests are seated, toss the contents of the pot onto the freezer paper and enjoy! Crab boil is available in seafood or gourmet markets.

Steamed Fish in Spinach Leaves

1 cup light cream
½ cup white wine
Juice of 1 lemon
1 teaspoon dried tarragon
¼ cup butter

½ bunch spinach, washed and stems trimmed
Water
1 halibut, swordfish, or shark steak, cut into 1½ × 1½-inch cubes
Paprika for garnish

Combine cream, wine, lemon juice, and tarragon and bring to a boil. Reduce to half. Set aside and keep warm. Mix in butter just before serving.

Place half of the spinach leaves in a steamer filled with about ½-inch water. Place cubed fish on spinach and cover completely with remaining spinach leaves. Cover and steam over medium heat for 15 to 20 minutes depending on amount of fish.

Uncover the steamed fish and test for doneness (do not overcook the fish). Replace spinach and place steamer on a paper towel to drain. Dab spinach with a paper towel to absorb excess water. Turn steamed fish and spinach out onto a plate and top with sauce. Garnish with a sprinkle of paprika.

Preparation Time: 30 minutes
Cooking Time: 15 to 20 minutes
Serves: 1

Poultry

Tortilla Pastel con Pollo
(Tortilla Pie with Chicken)

Cumin powder is from a plant found in the Mediterranean. It is a member of the carrot family used in Chinese, Spanish, and Mexican cooking for its spicy warm flavor.

5 whole chicken breasts, halved, boned, and skinned
Water
3 tablespoons ground cumin
1 bay leaf
1 large yellow onion, chopped
3 tablespoons olive oil
6 cloves garlic, minced
4 cups tomato sauce
1 cup tomato paste
3 tablespoons chili powder

2 teaspoons cayenne pepper
1 teaspoon ground oregano
¼ teaspoon pepper
12 green onions, chopped, ½ cup reserved for garnish
2 dozen corn tortillas
2 cups shredded Cheddar cheese
2 cups shredded Monterey jack cheese
Sour cream to serve

Place chicken in a large pot with enough water to cover by 1-inch. Add 2 tablespoons cumin and bay leaf to the water. Bring to a boil. Reduce heat and simmer for 20 minutes. Drain, reserving 2 cups of the seasoned broth. Set chicken aside to cool.

Sauté half of the yellow onion in olive oil in a large skillet over medium heat, until tender. Add garlic and sauté briefly. Add the tomato sauce, tomato paste, chili powder, remaining 1 tablespoon cumin, cayenne pepper, oregano, and pepper. Stir and bring to a boil. Reduce heat and add 2 cups of the reserved seasoned broth. Simmer for 30 minutes. Shred chicken. Combine remaining yellow onion with the green onions and set aside.

Preheat oven to 350 degrees.

Spoon a thin layer of the sauce into a 9 × 13-inch baking dish and spread evenly. Dip each tortilla in the sauce, coating thinly but evenly, and line the bottom of the dish (tortillas should overlap). Combine the cheeses. Layer half of the chicken, half of the yellow and green onion mixture, and 1½ cups of the combined cheeses. Spoon a little of the sauce over it and spread evenly. Repeat the process. Finish with a layer of dipped tortillas and the remaining sauce poured over the top. Sprinkle with the remaining 1 cup of combined cheeses and bake for 20 to 25 minutes or until bubbly. Garnish with the reserved green onions sprinkled over the top. Serve with sour cream.

Preparation Time: 35 to 40 minutes
Cooking Time: 25 to 30 minutes
Serves: 4 to 6

Shredded Chicken in Red Chile Sauce with Chèvre

3½ to 4 pounds chicken, cut up
Salt
Pepper
2 pasilla chiles (green)
3 dried red chile pods
1 cup hot chicken broth
1 large onion, diced
3 cloves garlic, minced

1 medium green bell pepper, diced
1 medium red bell pepper, diced
1 to 2 jalapeño peppers, stemmed, seeded, and diced
¾ cup mild California or French goat cheese
12 flour tortillas, warmed to serve

Preheat oven to 350 degrees.

Place chicken pieces in a baking dish and cover with foil. Bake for 30 minutes. Remove from oven and keep covered while cooling. Skin, bone, and shred chicken. Season with salt and pepper. Set aside.

Stem and seed the chiles and chop. Soak the pasilla and dried chiles in the hot chicken broth for 30 minutes. Pour chiles and the liquid into a food processor. Add onion, garlic, and bell peppers. Process until coarse. Place mixture in saucepan and simmer sauce for 15 minutes. Season with salt and pepper. Stir in diced jalapeño peppers. Spread 1 cup of sauce in the bottom of a baking dish. Layer chicken over sauce and top with remaining sauce. Crumble goat cheese over top and bake for 25 minutes or until sauce is bubbly. Serve with warm flour tortillas.

Preparation Time: 1 hour
Cooking Time: 55 minutes (includes time for cooking chicken)
Serves: 6

Note: May substitute feta cheese for goat cheese for a milder flavor.

Chicken Fajitas

2 whole chicken breasts, halved, boned, skinned, and sliced into long thin strips

¼ cup fresh lime juice

½ cup oil

1 medium green bell pepper, sliced into long thin strips

1 medium red bell pepper, sliced into long thin strips

½ red onion, sliced and pulled apart into single rings

8 to 10 green onions, chopped

3 cloves garlic, minced

Freshly ground pepper

1 teaspoon ground cumin

8 flour tortillas, 6-inch size to serve

2 ripe tomatoes, chopped to serve

2 cups chopped iceberg lettuce to serve

Salsa Fresca to serve (recipe page 147)

Guacamole to serve (recipe page 40)

Fresh chopped cilantro to serve

Place chicken in a shallow dish and pour lime juice over all. Set aside at room temperature for 1 hour.

Heat a wok or deep skillet to high with ¼ cup oil. Sauté bell peppers and red onion for 1 minute, tossing frequently. Remove mixture from skillet. Add the remaining ¼ cup oil and bring temperature back to high. Drain chicken and place in skillet. Add green onions, garlic, pepper, and cumin. Toss frequently, cooking for 3 to 4 minutes or until chicken is no longer pink. Reduce heat to low and add bell pepper mixture. Cover and steam for 1 minute. Warm tortillas. Serve chicken mixture, warm tortillas, and condiments buffet style.

Preparation Time: 1 hour 30 minutes

Cooking Time: 10 minutes

Serves: 4 to 6

Phyllo Chicken Pockets

1 cup chopped green onions	10 tablespoons butter, melted
1 cup mayonnaise	12 sheets phyllo dough
4 tablespoons fresh lemon juice	3 whole chicken breasts, halved, boned, and skinned
3 cloves garlic, minced	
1 tablespoon fresh tarragon	2 tablespoons grated Parmesan cheese
Salt	
Pepper	

Combine onions, mayonnaise, lemon juice, ⅔ of the garlic, tarragon, salt, and pepper. Set aside. Combine remaining garlic with melted butter. Brush 1 phyllo sheet with melted garlic butter. Place second sheet on top of first sheet, brush with garlic butter, and sprinkle with salt and pepper.

Preheat oven to 375 degrees.

Place chicken on a flat surface and spread 1 tablespoon of the mayonnaise mixture on 1 side only. Place chicken, mayonnaise side down, onto prepared phyllo sheets. Add 1 tablespoon of mayonnaise mixture on top of chicken and wrap up in phyllo. Repeat process until each chicken pocket is completed. Place pockets slightly apart, seam side down, in an unoiled baking dish. Brush with garlic butter and sprinkle with Parmesan cheese. Bake for 20 to 25 minutes.

Preparation Time: 20 minutes

Cooking Time: 20 to 25 minutes

Serves: 4 to 6

Note: To freeze, pack a single layer of pockets in a tightly sealed container. Thaw completely before baking.

Chicken Apple Sauté

4 tablespoons butter

2 large tart apples, peeled, cored, and
   cut into ¼-inch slices

1½ teaspoons cinnamon

2 whole chicken breasts, halved and
   boned

1 onion, sliced

⅔ cup dry sherry or apple juice

⅓ cup heavy cream

½ teaspoon salt

½ teaspoon white pepper

Melt 2 tablespoons butter in a skillet over medium heat. Add apple slices and ½ teaspoon cinnamon. Sauté, stirring frequently until just tender, about 1 to 2 minutes. Set aside and keep warm.

Increase heat to medium high and add remaining butter to pan. Add chicken and brown for about 5 minutes on each side until golden. Remove chicken from pan, set aside, and keep warm.

Add onion to pan juices and sauté, stirring occasionally until golden. Add sherry and sauté for 1 minute longer. Return chicken to pan, skin side up. Cover, reduce heat, and simmer until chicken is no longer pink.

Arrange breasts on a platter and top with apple slices. Stir cream into pan juices and add salt, ½ teaspoon cinnamon, and pepper. Increase heat to high. Bring to a boil. Boil uncovered until surface is covered with shiny bubbles and sauce is reduced by a third. Pour sauce over chicken and apples. Garnish with a sprinkle of the remaining cinnamon.

Preparation Time: 15 minutes

Cooking Time: 25 minutes

Serves: 3 to 4

Chilled Chicken in Yogurt Herb Sauce

**2 whole chicken breasts, halved,
   boned, and skinned**
1½ cups chicken broth
1 egg yolk
2 tablespoons lemon juice
1 teaspoon salt
¼ teaspoon pepper
½ teaspoon ground cumin

½ cup fresh parsley, firmly packed
**½ cup chopped fresh spinach leaves,
   firmly packed**
½ cup walnuts
¼ cup olive oil, extra virgin
¾ cup plain yogurt
Parsley sprigs for garnish

Poach chicken in broth for 8 to 10 minutes. Remove chicken and place in a 9 × 13-inch ceramic or glass baking dish.

Blend egg yolk, lemon juice, salt, pepper, and cumin in a food processor. Add parsley, spinach, and nuts. Blend for about 15 seconds. Add oil in a thin stream with motor running. Add yogurt and blend until smooth. Pour yogurt mixture over chicken. Chill for at least 2 hours, covered loosely, turning pieces occasionally. Chill overnight for added flavor. Garnish with parsley sprigs.

Preparation Time: 15 minutes
Cooking Time: 8 to 10 minutes
Serves: 3 to 4

Note: Slice chicken breasts into strips for an alternative serving suggestion.

Chicken and Avocados in Cognac Cream

Wine Suggestion:
Chardonnay or
Sauvignon Blanc

3 whole chicken breasts, halved,
    boned, and skinned
½ teaspoon salt
½ teaspoon pepper
3 tablespoons butter
1 tablespoon finely chopped shallots

¼ pound mushrooms, sliced
½ cup Cognac
1½ cups heavy cream
1 firm but ripe avocado, peeled,
    seeded, and cut into ½-inch
    slices

Cut each chicken breast into 6 strips. Sprinkle with salt and pepper. Heat butter in a heavy skillet. Add the chicken and cook over high heat, stirring and shaking the skillet until chicken is browned, approximately 3 to 4 minutes. Remove chicken with a slotted spoon and set aside. Reduce temperature. Add shallots and mushrooms to the skillet. Sauté briefly, stirring constantly. Sprinkle Cognac over the shallots and mushrooms. Stir in the cream and cook until thick. Season with salt and pepper. Return chicken to skillet. Add avocado gently and warm through, taking care not to break up avocado.

Preparation Time: 30 minutes

Cooking Time: 15 minutes

Serves: 6

Lemon Caper Chicken

Capers are found on
a low prickly shrub
indigenous to the
Mediterranean
region. The greenish
flower buds or young
berries of the caper
are pickled for use as
a relish.

Wine Suggestion:
Chardonnay or
Pinot Noir

Chicken and
Avocados in
Cognac Cream.

4 whole chicken breasts, halved,
    boned, and skinned
½ cup butter
4 cloves garlic, minced

½ pound fresh mushrooms, sliced
3 dashes Tabasco sauce
¼ cup fresh lemon juice
3 ounces capers, drained

Sauté chicken breasts in butter until golden. Remove from skillet to a warm platter. Add garlic and mushrooms to butter in skillet and sauté. Add Tabasco sauce, lemon juice, and capers. Stir over medium heat. Return chicken to the skillet and cook for approximately 20 minutes or until chicken is heated through.

Preparation Time: 30 minutes

Cooking Time: 20 minutes

Serves: 4

Note: Do not prepare in advance. Best if made just prior to serving.

Thai Chicken

3 tablespoons peanut oil
3½ pounds frying chicken, cut into serving pieces
1 whole bulb garlic, approximately 12 to 14 cloves, minced
2 dried hot red chile peppers or 1 teaspoon dried red pepper flakes

¾ cup white vinegar
¼ cup soy sauce
3 tablespoons honey
Cilantro sprigs for garnish
Chopped peanuts to serve
Julienned green onions to serve

Heat oil in a large heavy skillet and brown chicken well on all sides. Add garlic and peppers towards the end of browning the chicken. Combine remaining ingredients and add to the chicken. Cook over medium heat until chicken is done and sauce is somewhat reduced, about 10 minutes. Add a little water if necessary. Garnish with cilantro sprigs. Serve with peanuts and green onions.

Preparation Time: 10 minutes

Cooking Time: 25 minutes

Serves: 4 to 6

Apricot Chutney Chicken

5 whole chicken breasts, halved, boned, and skinned
3 tablespoons flour
2 tablespoons oil
2 cups Apricot Chutney (recipe page 189)
½ teaspoon cayenne pepper

2 cloves garlic, crushed
½ teaspoon salt
½ teaspoon pepper
½ cup dry white wine
½ cup chicken broth
1 teaspoon curry powder
1 teaspoon ground ginger

Preheat oven to 325 degrees.

Coat chicken lightly with flour. Heat oil in a large skillet. Add chicken pieces and brown on all sides. Drain chicken and place in a 9 × 13-inch baking dish. Blend remaining ingredients together. Pour sauce over chicken. Bake for 30 minutes or to desired doneness.

Preparation Time: 10 minutes

Cooking Time: 30 minutes

Serves: 6 to 8

Apricot Chutney

Chutney is a piquant blend of fruits, vegetables, spices, sugar, and vinegar. It is a type of relish varying from hot and spicy to mild and tangy.

1 pound dried apricots, cut into fourths
4 cups boiling water
8 cloves garlic
1 2-inch piece fresh ginger, peeled and coarsely chopped

1¼ cups red wine vinegar
2 cups sugar
¼ teaspoon salt
½ teaspoon cayenne pepper
¾ cup golden raisins
Canning jars and lids

Place apricots in a large bowl and pour boiling water over apricots. Soak for 2 hours.

Combine garlic, ginger, and ¼ cup red wine vinegar in food processor. Process until smooth. Combine apricots and garlic mixture in heavy pan (not aluminum). Add remaining vinegar, sugar, salt, and cayenne pepper. Bring to a boil and simmer over medium heat for 45 minutes, stirring frequently (do not let it stick to bottom of pan). Lower heat if necessary. Add raisins and cook for another 30 minutes or until chutney has thickened and has a glazed look. Pour into canning jars that have been boiled. Top with lid and invert while cooling to insure better seal.

Preparation Time: 2 hours 30 minutes (includes soaking time)
Cooking Time: 1 hour 15 minutes
Makes: 4 cups

Mu Shu Chicken California

2 whole chicken breasts, boned,
  skinned, and diced
¼ cup dry sherry
1 tablespoon soy sauce
1 teaspoon cornstarch
1 teaspoon sugar
Pepper
5 to 6 large dried oyster or shitake
  mushrooms, soaked for 20
  minutes in hot water to cover (1
  cup sliced fresh mushrooms may
  be used)
1 cup dried tiger lily buds (Golden
  Needles), soaked for 20 minutes
  in hot water to cover

¼ cup peanut oil
1 tablespoon minced ginger
6 eggs, beaten
4 green onions, sliced in 1-inch pieces
2 cups fresh bean sprouts
2 cups shredded Chinese cabbage
2 tablespoons sesame oil
Soy sauce
6 to 8 flour tortillas or Chinese
  pancakes
Plum Sauce (recipe page 191)

Combine chicken, sherry, soy sauce, cornstarch, sugar, and pepper in a medium bowl. Marinate for 30 minutes, stirring occasionally.

Drain and rinse mushrooms and tiger lily buds. Cut away any tough portions of the mushrooms, usually the stem, and of the tiger lily buds, usually the tips. Slice the mushrooms into strips and cut the tiger lily buds into 1-inch long pieces. Set aside.

Heat 2 tablespoons peanut oil in a wok or skillet over medium heat. Add minced ginger and heat until golden. Add eggs and scramble until soft. Remove and set aside. Add 1 tablespoon peanut oil to the wok or skillet and cook chicken until done. Remove and set aside. Add 1 tablespoon peanut oil to the wok or skillet and bring up the temperature. Add green onions, mushrooms, and tiger lily buds. Cook for 3 minutes, stirring constantly. Add bean sprouts and cabbage and cook for 3 minutes, stirring constantly. Return eggs to the wok or skillet. Add sesame oil and toss. Add chicken, sprinkle with soy sauce, and toss until heated through.

Steam or warm flour tortillas or Chinese pancakes. Brush with Plum Sauce and place ½ to ¾ cup chicken mixture in center of tortilla or pancake and roll like a burrito. Top with warm Plum Sauce.

Preparation Time: 50 minutes

Cooking Time: 20 minutes

Serves: 4 to 6

Plum Sauce

16 ounces dark plum preserves
1 tablespoon cider vinegar
¼ cup sherry
1 1-inch cube fresh ginger, peeled and
finely minced
2 cloves garlic, finely minced

1 teaspoon salt
2 teaspoons chili powder
2 tablespoons mild diced green chiles
1 cup hoison sauce

Combine ingredients in a small saucepan. Cook over low heat until preserves melt, stirring constantly. Pour into a blender and blend until smooth. Cool sauce and refrigerate in covered container until ready to use. Serve warm or at room temperature.

Preparation Time: 10 minutes

Cooking Time: 5 minutes

Makes: 2½ cups

Note: Plum Sauce will keep for several weeks in the refrigerator. Hoison sauce may be found in the oriental section of most grocery stores.

Chicken Veronique

The term "Veronique" refers to any dish garnished with seedless green grapes.

4 whole chicken breasts, halved,
boned, and skinned
Salt
2 tablespoons butter
1½ tablespoons orange marmalade
½ teaspoon dried tarragon leaves

½ cup sherry
½ cup heavy cream
2 teaspoons cornstarch
Water
1½ cups seedless green grapes

Sprinkle chicken lightly with salt. Melt butter in a skillet over medium heat. Add chicken, browning lightly on each side. Top each breast with equal portions of marmalade. Add tarragon and sherry. Cover and simmer for 20 minutes or until thoroughly cooked. Transfer chicken to a serving dish and keep warm. Add cream to pan juices and blend well. Bring to a boil quickly. Blend cornstarch with enough water to make a thick paste. Add paste to sauce and return to a boil. Stir in grapes and heat gently. Pour sauce over chicken and serve.

Preparation Time: 15 minutes

Cooking Time: 10 minutes

Serves: 4

Oven Barbeque Chicken

2 tablespoons butter
3 cloves garlic, minced
1 cup catsup
2 tablespoons brown sugar, packed
1 tablespoon Worcestershire sauce

1 teaspoon salt
¼ teaspoon pepper
1 teaspoon Tabasco sauce
4 whole chicken breasts, halved
1 onion, sliced into rings

Prepare sauce at least 2 hours 30 minutes before using. Combine butter, garlic, catsup, brown sugar, Worcestershire sauce, salt, pepper, and Tabasco sauce in a saucepan. Bring to a boil. Reduce heat and simmer for 10 minutes.

Preheat oven to 375 degrees.

Place chicken in a 9×13-inch baking dish. Top with onion rings. Cover with sauce. Bake for 1 hour or to desired doneness.

Preparation Time: 10 minutes
Cooking Time: 1 hour
Serves: 4 to 6

Note: A zesty dish that is simple to prepare. Add more Tabasco sauce for additional spice.

Grilled Honey Chicken

½ cup butter
⅓ cup vinegar
½ cup honey
3 cloves garlic, minced
1 teaspoon salt
1 teaspoon dry mustard

½ teaspoon dried marjoram leaves
Pepper
¼ cup fresh orange juice
1 teaspoon cornstarch
3 whole chicken breasts, halved and boned

Preheat oven to 250 degrees.

Combine all ingredients except the chicken in a saucepan and bring to a boil. Place chicken in a shallow baking dish. Pour marinade over chicken. Marinate chicken for 2 hours. Bake chicken for 15 minutes. Finish cooking chicken on a grill to desired doneness.

Preparation Time: 15 minutes plus 2 hours marinating time
Cooking Time: 15 minutes plus grill time
Serves: 4 to 6

Note: Chicken may be sliced into strips and put on skewers. Brush with marinade while grilling. May be broiled as well.

Roasted Rosemary Chicken

Wine Suggestion:
Chardonnay or
Pinot Noir

1 roasting chicken
2 tablespoons fresh lemon juice
1 tablespoon dried rosemary, crushed
1 clove garlic, minced

1 teaspoon onion powder
1 apple, quartered
1 onion, quartered
1 stalk celery, halved

Preheat oven to 350 degrees.

Wash and pat chicken dry. Remove giblets and discard. Brush chicken with lemon juice. Sprinkle chicken inside and out with crushed rosemary, garlic, and onion powder. Place apple, onion, and celery in cavity. Bake for approximately 1 hour 30 minutes uncovered. Discard cavity stuffing. Allow bird to rest for 5 minutes before carving.

Preparation Time: 10 minutes

Cooking Time: 1 hour 30 minutes

Serves: 4

Note: A classic roasted chicken that is delicious and simple.

Champagne Chicken

Wine Suggestion:
Champagne or
Chardonnay

Roasted Rosemary Chicken; Green Beans with Orange Sauce.

3 whole chicken breasts, halved and boned
12 ounces cream cheese, softened
3 tablespoons sliced almonds, toasted

3 tablespoons golden raisins
¼ cup chopped chives
1 cup champagne
Chopped chives for garnish

Preheat oven to 325 degrees.

Pound chicken slightly to ¼ to ½-inch thickness. Spread cream cheese generously over chicken. Top with almonds, raisins, and a few chives. Roll up and place in a baking dish, seam side down. Pour champagne over top. Bake for 35 to 40 minutes uncovered. Add more champagne if needed. Garnish with chives.

Preparation Time: 10 minutes

Cooking Time: 40 minutes

Serves: 4 to 6

Country Wrapped Chicken

3 whole chicken breasts, halved, boned, and skinned
1 egg, beaten
¼ cup milk
¾ cup seasoned bread crumbs

¼ cup grated Parmesan cheese
6 thick slices Monterey jack or mozzarella cheese, cut into 3-inch strips
6 to 12 slices bacon

Preheat oven to 350 degrees.

Pound chicken breasts slightly. Beat egg and milk together in a shallow dish. Combine bread crumbs and Parmesan cheese in another shallow dish. Dip chicken in egg mixture and then in bread crumbs. Place 1 slice of cheese in the middle of each breast and roll up chicken. Wrap chicken in 1 or 2 slices of bacon. Roll in bread crumb mixture. Place in a baking dish and bake for approximately 30 to 40 minutes or to desired doneness. Drain on a paper towel to absorb extra bacon droppings.

Preparation Time: 25 minutes

Cooking Time: 30 to 40 minutes

Serves: 4

Note: If bacon slices are thick, precook until transparent. Freezes well before baking.

Chicken with Currant Glaze

½ cup fresh currants (or dried)

1¾ cups water

1½ cups currant jelly

1 tablespoon cornstarch (mixed with enough water to make a smooth paste)

1½ teaspoons ground allspice

1 tablespoon Worcestershire sauce

2 tablespoons lemon juice

Salt

Pepper

4 whole chicken breasts, halved and boned

¼ cup oil

Plump currants, if dried, in 1 cup water for 5 minutes. Drain water from currants. Combine remaining ingredients except chicken and oil in a small saucepan. Bring to a boil. Remove from heat.

Preheat oven to 350 degrees.

Brown chicken in oil. Place chicken in an uncovered 9 × 13-inch baking dish. Pour 3 tablespoons of sauce over each chicken breast. Bake for 35 to 40 minutes or to desired doneness. Place on a platter and spoon over remaining sauce. Serve immediately.

Preparation Time: 10 minutes

Cooking Time: 40 minutes

Serves: 6 to 8

Cheddared Chicken

4 whole chicken breasts, halved and boned

3 tablespoons Dijon mustard

1 tablespoon chopped fresh thyme or 1 teaspoon dried

Salt

Pepper

4 to 6 green onions, cut into 2-inch lengths, divided into 8 bunches

8 ounces sharp Cheddar cheese, cut into 8 sticks

2 tablespoons butter

¾ cup brandy

¾ cup heavy cream

Thyme sprigs for garnish

Pound chicken to ¼ to ½-inch thickness. Spread 1 teaspoon Dijon mustard on each breast. Sprinkle each breast with thyme, salt, and pepper. Lay 1 bunch of green onions and 1 cheese stick in center of chicken breast. Roll up breasts and secure with woodpicks. Brown breasts in butter in a large skillet. Add brandy to the pan. Cover and simmer over medium heat for 15 minutes. Remove breasts and keep warm. Stir in cream and simmer until sauce is reduced and thickened. Remove woodpicks. Top chicken breasts with sauce and serve garnished with thyme sprigs.

Preparation Time: 30 minutes

Cooking Time: 15 minutes

Serves: 6 to 8

Spanish Soft Tacos

1 whole chicken, cut up
    (approximately 3 to 4 pounds)
Salt
Pepper
12 ounces white corn
8 ounces creamed corn
2 ounces diced mild green chiles
½ cup slivered almonds
1 cup raisins
½ cup grated onion
2 teaspoons chili powder
½ teaspoon ground cumin
1 teaspoon salt
½ teaspoon pepper
¼ teaspoon cayenne pepper
2 cups sour cream
2 teaspoons Worcestershire sauce
2 cups shredded Monterey jack
    cheese
12 flour tortillas
Sour cream

Preheat oven to 350 degrees.

Sprinkle chicken pieces with salt and pepper. Place in a large glass baking dish. Cover with foil and bake for 30 minutes or until tender. Cool chicken. Skin, bone, and shred chicken. Combine chicken, white corn, creamed corn, green chiles, almonds, raisins, onion, chili powder, cumin, salt, pepper, cayenne pepper, sour cream, and Worcestershire sauce in a baking dish. Sprinkle with cheese and bake for 45 minutes. Spoon onto warm flour tortillas. Top each with a generous dollop of sour cream. Serve folded over or rolled up.

Preparation Time: 1 hour
Cooking Time: 1 hour 10 minutes
Serves: 6 to 8

Note: Chicken may be prepared ahead of time. If only breast meat is desired, use 4 whole chicken breasts. This is a gourmet alternative to the basic chicken taco.

Confetti Filled Blue Corn Cups

Confetti Filled Blue
Corn Cups are a
favorite creation of
P.K. Sheldon at Ma
Cuisine.

Corn Cups

6 ounces cream cheese, softened

¾ cup unsalted butter, softened

½ cup sour cream

2 cups flour

1 cup blue cornmeal

¼ teaspoon salt

Preheat oven to 350 degrees.

Combine cream cheese, butter, and sour cream until well blended. Combine flour, cornmeal, and salt. Add flour mixture to cream cheese mixture a little at a time, stirring by hand. Knead lightly. Press 1-inch balls into small muffin cups to form cups. Bake for 20 minutes.

Cilantro Pesto

2 cloves garlic, peeled

4 ounces grated Parmesan cheese, room temperature

⅓ cup pine nuts

2 cups fresh cilantro leaves

5 to 6 tablespoons olive oil

Salt

Pepper

Drop garlic and Parmesan cheese through feed tube of a food processor while motor is running. Process until coarse. Add nuts, cilantro, and oil. Blend until mixture is well combined. Season with salt and pepper.

Filling

1 whole breast of chicken

1 cup chicken broth

1 red bell pepper, roasted, peeled, and diced

1 ear corn, remove corn from cob

1 zucchini, diced

1 small jícama, diced

Salt

Freshly ground pepper

Cilantro Pesto (recipe above)

Poach chicken breast in broth until done. Remove to cool. Add vegetables to remaining broth. Cook slowly for 10 minutes. Season with salt and pepper. Dice cooled chicken and add to vegetables. Stir in Cilantro Pesto to taste. Fill warm corn cups and serve.

Preparation Time: 1 hour

Cooking Time: 1 hour

Makes: 9 cups

Note: May omit chicken for a vegetable side dish.

Braised Quail

Wine Suggestion:
Pinot Noir or Gamay

6 to 8 quail
Salt
Freshly ground pepper
½ cup butter
2 slices onion

1 tablespoon flour
¾ cup wine
¾ cup chicken broth
1 cup sliced mushrooms

Sprinkle birds with salt and generous grinds of pepper (remove neck and wings if desired). Melt butter in a large skillet and sauté onion until tender. Remove onion with a slotted spoon and set aside. Place birds in a skillet and brown on all sides. Remove birds and set aside.

Preheat oven to 275 degrees.

Add flour to the butter, blending well, and cook for about 1 minute. Stir in wine and chicken broth. Return birds and onion to pan and cover. Bake for 1 hour 15 minutes, turning birds every 30 minutes. Add mushrooms to the pan for the last 30 minutes of cooking.

Preparation Time: 20 minutes
Cooking Time: 1 hour 15 minutes
Serves: 2 to 4

Roast Duck with Three Berry Sauce

Wine Suggestion:
Pinot Noir or Merlot

Roast Duck
2 6-pound domestic ducks
1 apple, chopped
1 onion, chopped
2 stalks chopped celery
Three Berry Sauce to serve (recipe below)

Preheat oven to 375 degrees.

Remove giblets from the cavity of each duck. Rinse ducks inside and out. Combine the apple, onion, and celery. Stuff cavities of ducks with the apple, onion, and celery mixture. Roast ducks breast side up for 3 hours or 30 minutes for each pound or to desired doneness. Allow ducks to rest for about 10 minutes before carving. Serve with Three Berry Sauce.

Three Berry Sauce
1 cup beef broth
½ cup Sauterne
4 tablespoons brown sugar
3 tablespoons raspberry vinegar
½ cup orange marmalade
1⅓ cups strawberries, hulled and halved
1⅓ cups blackberries
1⅓ cups raspberries
2 tablespoons cornstarch
3 tablespoons orange juice

Heat broth, Sauterne, sugar, vinegar, and marmalade in a saucepan, stirring until the sugar is dissolved and the marmalade is melted. Purée 1 cup each of strawberries, blackberries, and raspberries with the broth mixture in a blender or food processor. Return purée to saucepan. Dissolve cornstarch in orange juice and stir into purée. Add the remaining ⅓ cup of each berry to the purée mixture. Bring to a boil over medium-high heat, stirring for 1 minute. Remove from heat and serve.

Preparation Time: 45 minutes

Cooking Time: 3 hours

Serves: 4 to 6

Note: The sauce is delicious served with Crispy Cinnamon Logs (recipe page 133).

Preceding pages feature:
Roast Duck with Three Berry Sauce;
Minted Wild Rice Salad.

Roasted Cornish Game Hens with White Grapes

Wine Suggestion:
Chardonnay or Pinot
Noir

2 Cornish game hens
6 tablespoons butter
Salt
Freshly ground pepper
30 Thompson seedless grapes, halved
4 to 5 tablespoons Cognac

¼ cup sherry
1 cup chicken broth
1½ teaspoons arrowroot
1 tablespoon grated lemon zest
1 tablespoon lemon juice

Preheat oven to 350 degrees.

Remove giblets from hens. Rub hens generously with butter and sprinkle with salt and pepper. Put 1 tablespoon butter in each cavity. Sprinkle each cavity with salt and pepper. Place 3 to 4 grapes in each cavity. Sprinkle hens with 2 to 3 tablespoons Cognac. Place in a roasting pan and bake for about 1 hour 15 minutes. Baste the hens thoroughly 3 to 4 times during roasting.

Heat 2 tablespoons Cognac, sherry, broth, and remaining grapes gently in a small saucepan. Remove grapes with a slotted spoon and spoon around hens for the last 5 minutes of roasting time. Remove hens to a heated serving platter. Mix arrowroot into the warm broth mixture and add to roasting pan juices. Add lemon zest and lemon juice. Stir well, scraping up brown bits on bottom of pan, and simmer until slightly thickened. Cut hens in half. Pour sauce over hens and serve.

Preparation Time: 20 minutes

Cooking Time: 1 hour 15 minutes

Serves: 2

Note: Quail may be substituted for game hens. Roast 4 quail for 12 to 15 minutes at 450 degrees. Continue as above.

Turkey Medallions with Tequila Lime Sauce

Coriander is the seed of the Chinese parsley (cilantro) plant. It is an Old World herb of the carrot family. It has a delicate texture and a surprisingly sweet yet pungent flavor.

8 turkey medallions, approximately 1½ pounds, or 1½ to 2 pounds turkey breast, boned and sliced into 4-ounce slices
4 tablespoons butter
¼ cup fresh lime juice
¼ cup plus 1 tablespoon gold tequila
⅓ cup heavy cream

¼ teaspoon ground coriander
2 tablespoons chopped fresh cilantro
2 tablespoons chopped fresh chives
¼ teaspoon salt
¼ teaspoon pepper
Cilantro sprigs for garnish

Pound each medallion between sheets of wax paper to ⅛-inch thickness. Heat 2 tablespoons butter in a large skillet and sauté the turkey over medium-high heat until golden brown, about 2 minutes on each side. Transfer to a platter and keep warm. Add lime juice and tequila to the skillet and simmer for about 3 minutes. Add remaining butter and stir until smooth. Stir in cream and coriander and simmer for another 3 minutes. Add cilantro, chives, salt, and pepper and stir. Remove from heat. Pour sauce over turkey medallions. Garnish with sprigs of cilantro.

Preparation Time: 30 minutes
Cooking Time: 20 minutes
Serves: 4

Note: This recipe provides a tangy blend of Southwestern flavors.

Turkey Scallopini with Currant Citrus Sauce

Wine Suggestion:
Gewürtztraminer or
Reisling

Turkey Scallopini

8 turkey scallops, approximately 1½ pounds, or 1½ to 2 pounds turkey breast, boned and sliced into ¼-inch slices

1 cup crushed cornflakes

½ cup sesame seeds

2 tablespoons chopped fresh parsley

¼ cup grated Parmesan cheese

½ teaspoon pepper

4 tablespoons melted butter

Preheat oven to 425 degrees. Lightly oil a baking sheet.

Pound each scallop between sheets of wax paper to ¼-inch thickness. Combine cornflakes, sesame seeds, parsley, Parmesan cheese, and pepper. Dip turkey into melted butter and coat with cornflake mixture. Place on the prepared baking sheet and bake for 15 to 20 minutes.

Citrus Sauce

¾ cup fresh orange juice

¾ cup fresh lemon juice

½ cup currant jelly

1 tablespoon white wine

1 tablespoon Dijon mustard

½ teaspoon ground ginger

3 tablespoons dried currants

1 teaspoon grated lemon peel

1 teaspoon grated orange peel

2 tablespoons butter

2 tablespoons cornstarch

Fresh lemon slices for garnish

Fresh orange slices for garnish

Combine all sauce ingredients except butter and cornstarch in a saucepan and warm over low heat. Melt butter in a separate pan. Add cornstarch and blend until smooth. Slowly add the cornstarch mixture to the sauce mixture and cook until thickened, stirring constantly. Place turkey on a platter and top with sauce. Garnish with lemon and orange slices.

Preparation Time: 30 minutes

Cooking Time: 20 minutes

Serves: 4

Roast Turkey with Raisin Pine Nut Stuffing

1 12 to 14-pound turkey
Salt
Freshly ground pepper

1 recipe Raisin Pine Nut Stuffing
    (recipe page 209)
½ cup butter

Preheat oven to 350 degrees.

Remove giblets from cavity of turkey. Rinse turkey inside and out. Pat dry. Sprinkle inside and out with salt and pepper. Fill cavity with completely cooled stuffing. Place any remaining stuffing in neck under flap. Truss turkey. Place turkey breast side up on a rack in a large roasting pan and brush with melted butter. Roast, basting frequently, for about 3 hours to 3 hours 30 minutes, until a thermometer inserted in the thickest part of a thigh registers 170 to 175 degrees. Discard skewers or string and remove stuffing from cavity and place in a serving dish. Allow turkey to rest for about 10 minutes before carving.

Preparation Time: 1 hour (includes stuffing preparation)
Cooking Time: 3 hours to 3 hours 30 minutes
Serves: 8

Raisin Pine Nut Stuffing

4 cups dry bread cubes (made from French bread, cut into 1-inch cubes)

½ cup raisins

½ cup tequila

2 large red bell peppers

2 large Anaheim chiles

½ cup butter

1 large onion, chopped

2 large cloves garlic, minced

2 stalks celery, chopped

¼ cup chopped fresh cilantro

1 teaspoon salt

1½ teaspoons oregano

1 teaspoon California chili powder or chili powder

2 teaspoons dried sage

Freshly ground pepper

1½ cups toasted pine nuts

½ cup chicken broth

Spread bread cubes on a baking sheet and allow to dry for several hours. Toss bread cubes a few times during the day to dry on all sides.

Plump raisins in tequila for 30 minutes. Blacken bell peppers and chiles over a gas flame or under a broiler 6-inches from heat, on all sides, for about 10 minutes. Place in a brown paper bag and allow to stand for 10 minutes to steam. Peel and seed. Chop peppers and chiles coarsely.

Preheat oven to 350 degrees.

Drain raisins, discarding tequila. Melt butter in large skillet over medium-low heat. Add onion, garlic, and celery. Sauté, stirring often, until tender, about 10 minutes. Add bread cubes, cilantro, salt, oregano, chili powder, sage, and pepper. Fold in pine nuts, raisins, bell peppers, and chiles. Drizzle broth over bread mixture and toss until thoroughly moistened. Spoon into a 2-quart casserole and bake for 30 minutes or until heated through.

Preparation Time: 1 hour

Cooking Time: 30 minutes

Serves: 8 to 10

Note: An excellent side dish and a unique departure from the traditional turkey stuffing. For stuffing a turkey, refer to recipe page 208.

Meats

Veal Scallopini with Tarragon Mustard Sauce

Wine Suggestion:
Zinfandel or
Chardonnay

8 veal scallops, approximately 2 pounds
Flour
4 tablespoons butter
4 tablespoons olive oil
1 cup beef broth
2 tablespoons fresh or 1½ teaspoons dried tarragon

1 cup heavy cream
2 tablespoons Dijon mustard
2 tablespoons capers
Salt
Freshly ground pepper

Pound the veal to ¼-inch thickness and lightly flour. Shake off excess flour. Melt butter and heat oil in a large skillet over medium-high heat. Add veal and sauté until light brown, about 3 to 4 minutes per side. Transfer veal to a serving dish. Cover and keep warm. Skim fat from skillet. Add broth and tarragon to skillet and cook over high heat until reduced to 1 cup, about 10 minutes. Stir in cream and cook until thickened, about 3 to 4 minutes. Whisk in mustard and capers. Season with salt and pepper. Serve with sauce spooned over the top.

Preparation Time: 30 minutes

Cooking Time: 30 minutes

Serves: 4

Veal Scallops with Ginger and Lime

Zest is the oily,
aromatic, colored
part of the rind of
citrus fruits.

Wine Suggestion:
Gewürtztraminer or
Pinot Gris

3 tablespoons plus 2 teaspoons flour
Salt
Pepper
1 pound veal scallops, pounded thin
4 tablespoons unsalted butter,
   softened
½ cup white wine

½ cup chicken broth
Water
1 tablespoon minced ginger
1 tablespoon green peppercorns
2 teaspoons grated lime zest
2 tablespoons lime juice
Fresh lime slices for garnish

Season 3 tablespoons flour with salt and pepper. Lightly coat veal with seasoned flour. Melt 2 tablespoons butter in a large skillet over high heat. Add veal and sauté for 1 to 2 minutes per side or to desired doneness. Remove to a serving platter and keep warm. Add wine and broth to skillet. Simmer, scraping bottom of pan. Combine 2 teaspoons flour with enough water to make a smooth paste. Bring wine and broth to a boil and slowly add flour paste. Add ginger, peppercorns, lime zest, and juice. Simmer for 2 to 3 minutes. Whisk in remaining 2 tablespoons butter. Add salt and pepper. Pour sauce over veal. Garnish with lime slices.

Preparation Time: 20 minutes
Cooking Time: 5 to 10 minutes
Serves: 4

Note: For variation, use pink and green peppercorns. This is a wonderfully pungent sauce.

Veal Alfredo

¾ pound fresh fettucini or Pasta Fresca (recipe page 141)
Oil
1 cup unsalted butter
2½ cups light cream
¼ teaspoon cayenne pepper
1 cup grated Parmesan cheese
3 eggs

6 slices veal, pounded thin
¾ cup finely crushed dry bread crumbs
1½ tablespoons minced fresh parsley
1½ tablespoons olive oil
½ teaspoon white pepper
½ teaspoon onion powder
2 cloves garlic, pressed

Cook fettucini until tender but firm (al dente). Drain and toss with a few drops of oil to keep from sticking together. Set aside.

Melt butter in a saucepan over medium-low heat. Add cream and whisk constantly until it boils. Reduce to a simmer and continue whisking until thickened enough to coat a spoon, about 7 to 8 minutes. Remove from heat. Add cayenne pepper and ¾ cup Parmesan cheese. Whisk until cheese is melted and set aside.

Beat eggs in a pan. Add the remaining ¼ cup Parmesan cheese to the eggs. Soak veal in egg mixture for at least 5 minutes. Combine bread crumbs, parsley, olive oil, pepper, onion powder, and garlic in a shallow pan. Dredge the veal in the bread crumbs, coating well and pressing the crumbs in with your hands. Heat ¼-inch oil in a large skillet until very hot but not smoking. Sauté veal until golden brown, about 1 minute per side. Remove veal to a warm platter and set aside.

Reheat cheese sauce over medium-high heat, whisking often. Add fettucini and toss gently until thoroughly coated and heated through, about 1 minute. Serve veal over fettucini.

Preparation Time: 45 minutes
Cooking Time: 10 minutes
Serves: 6

Stuffed Crown Roast of Pork

Wine Suggestion:
Zinfandel or
Gewürztraminer

1 9 to 10-pound crown roast of pork
1¼ teaspoons salt
1 cup wild rice
1 cup white rice
1 cup finely chopped onion
1 pound mushrooms, sliced
3 cups finely diced cooked ham or
    Canadian bacon

¾ cup butter
1 teaspoon dried marjoram leaves,
    crushed
1 teaspoon dried thyme leaves,
    crushed
Pepper
Fresh tangerine or orange wedges for
    garnish

Preheat oven to 325 degrees.

Sprinkle meat lightly with ¼ teaspoon salt. Place roast in a shallow roasting pan lined with a triple thickness of heavy duty foil. Cover tips of ribs with foil to protect them from overbrowning during roasting. Insert a meat thermometer into the center of meat, away from fat and bone. Roast meat until thermometer reads 170 degrees, allowing about 20 minutes per pound, depending on the thickness of the ribs.

Rinse wild rice thoroughly and drain. Prepare wild rice and white rice separately, according to the package directions for each. Sauté onion, mushrooms, and ham in butter in a large skillet until onion is transparent. Add cooked rice to skillet. Season with remaining salt, marjoram, thyme, and pepper. Place half of stuffing in the center of the roast during the last hour of cooking. Bake remaining stuffing in a casserole during the last 45 minutes of roasting.

Remove roast from oven when the meat thermometer reaches 170 degrees. Remove aluminum foil covering the ribs. Slide foil from under roast once it is on the serving platter. Top each rib with a paper frill. Garnish with fresh tangerine or orange wedges.

Preparation Time: 1 hour
Cooking Time: Depends on size of roast. A 9-pound roast takes approximately
                    3 hours.
Serves: 8 to 10

Grilled Pork Tenderloin with Dijon Cornichon Sauce

Wine Suggestion:
*Pinot Gris or
Chardonnay*

2 pork tenderloins, about 2 to 3 pounds total
2 tablespoons oil
6 tablespoons butter, softened
4 tablespoons Dijon mustard
½ cup minced shallots
2 cups dry white wine

3 tablespoons minced fresh tarragon
2 tablespoons heavy cream
8 cornichons, julienned (may substitute gherkins)
Salt
Pepper

Preheat grill.

Bring tenderloins to room temperature. Brush tenderloins with oil and grill over hot coals for approximately 45 minutes to 1 hour or until thermometer registers 170 degrees.

Cream butter and mustard in small bowl. Set aside. Combine shallots, wine, and tarragon in a small saucepan. Cook over moderately high heat until wine is reduced to 6 tablespoons. Add cream and cornichons over low heat. Whisk in the mustard butter, adding small amounts at a time. Season with salt and pepper. Keep warm while slicing tenderloin. Top meat with sauce and serve.

Preparation Time: 15 minutes

Cooking Time: 45 minutes to 1 hour

Serves: 4

Note: Reduction of shallots, wine, and tarragon may be done the day prior. Store covered in refrigerator. Beef tenderloin may be substituted for pork.

Roast Pork Loin with Gingered Apricots

Ginger is the pungent, spicy root of a reedlike plant cultivated in most tropical countries.

1 2 to 3-pound pork loin roast
Salt
Pepper
1½ cups halved dried apricots
¾ cup apricot brandy
½ cup water
1 cup chicken broth
½ cup Triple Sec

1 1-inch cube ginger, peeled and cut into thin matchsticks
¼ cup orange marmalade
2 teaspoons Dijon mustard
Salt
Pepper
4 green onions, julienned and cut into 1-inch lengths for garnish

Preheat oven to 325 degrees.

Season roast with salt and pepper. Place in a roasting pan or baking dish and roast for 2 to 3 hours or until meat thermometer reads 170 degrees.

Soak apricots in ½ cup apricot brandy and water for 30 minutes, stirring occasionally. Place apricots and liquid in a large skillet. Simmer over medium heat for 5 minutes. Add broth, remaining ¼ cup apricot brandy, Triple Sec, ginger, marmalade, mustard, salt, and pepper. Simmer over low heat for 30 minutes, stirring occasionally. Cover and simmer over low heat for 10 minutes, stirring occasionally (do not let apricots stick). Remove from heat and keep covered until roast is done.

Place roast on a serving platter and spoon apricots over roast. Top with julienned green onions.

Preparation Time: 45 minutes
Cooking Time: 2 to 3 hours depending on size of roast
Serves: 4 to 6

Roast Pork Loin Stuffed with Fruit in a Cream Sauce

Wine Suggestion:
Zinfandel, Semillon,
or Gewürtztraminer

1 3-pound boneless pork roast
1 cup light cream
1 cup sour cream
2 teaspoons sugar
1 tablespoon sherry
½ cup golden raisins
½ cup chopped dried apricots
1 cup orange juice

2 cups herb seasoned stuffing mix
1 egg, beaten
5 tablespoons butter, melted
Salt
White pepper
¼ cup chicken broth
½ cup apricot jam, heated

Slice the pork roast lengthwise in half about ¾ of the way through (a butcher will do this best). Refrigerate until ready to prepare. Combine cream, sour cream, sugar, and sherry. Refrigerate overnight. Combine raisins and apricots in orange juice and refrigerate overnight.

Preheat oven to 350 degrees.

Pound roast flat, but not too thin. Drain the orange juice from the raisins and apricots. Combine raisin and apricot mixture, stuffing mix, egg, 3 tablespoons butter, scant salt, and pepper. Add only enough broth to hold the stuffing together. Sprinkle roast lightly with salt and pepper. Lay cut side of roast up and place stuffing mixture over the roast leaving about a ½ inch around the sides. Roll sides together, skewer, and tie with string (the roast should be in the shape of a roll). Place in a baking dish, seam side down. Bake for 1 hour 45 minutes. Combine apricot jam and remaining 2 tablespoons butter. Baste with jam mixture 3 times. Serve with warmed cream sauce.

Preparation Time: 35 minutes
Cooking Time: 1 hour 45 minutes
Serves: 4 to 6

**Roast Pork Loin
Stuffed with Fruit in
a Cream Sauce.**

Marinated Rib Eye Roast

1 5-pound boneless rib eye roast, trimmed

⅓ cup coarsely cracked pepper

½ teaspoon ground cardamon

1 cup soy sauce

¾ cup red wine vinegar

1 tablespoon tomato paste

1 teaspoon paprika

4 cloves garlic, minced

Fresh parsley sprigs for garnish

6 apricot halves for garnish

Jalapeño Pepper Jelly to serve (recipe page 103)

Preheat oven to 325 degrees.

Place the roast in a pan. Combine pepper and cardamon. Pat firmly onto roast. Combine soy sauce, vinegar, tomato paste, paprika, and garlic. Pour over roast. Cover and marinate overnight in refrigerator, turning occasionally.

Remove roast from marinade. Discard marinade. Wrap roast in foil and place in a shallow pan. Insert meat thermometer, keeping thermometer clear of foil. Bake for 2 hours or until thermometer registers 140 degrees for rare or 160 degrees for medium. Garnish with parsley and apricot halves, placing 1 to 2 teaspoons Jalapeño Pepper Jelly in hollows of apricot halves. Serve with Jalapeño Pepper Jelly.

Preparation Time: 45 minutes

Cooking Time: 2 hours

Serves: 6 to 8

Filet Mignon in Puff Pastry

Wine Suggestion:
Cabernet Sauvignon
or Merlot

1 5-pound beef tenderloin
1 cup sliced fresh mushrooms
2 tablespoons chopped fresh parsley
Salt
Pepper
3 cloves garlic, minced

½ cup brandy
¼ cup Dijon mustard
1 sheet puff pastry (11 × 14-inches)
1 egg
1 tablespoon water
Tarragon Hollandaise Sauce (recipe below)

Preheat oven to 500 degrees.

Brown tenderloin quickly on all sides in a heavy skillet. Remove from pan. Sauté mushrooms and parsley. Season with salt, pepper, and garlic. Slice tenderloin into 6 slices, cross-grain, ⅔ of the way through. Insert mushroom mixture between the slices. Return tenderloin to original shape. Brush tenderloin with brandy and mustard. Season with salt and pepper. Wrap with puff pastry. Bake tenderloin in oven for 5 minutes at 500 degrees. Reduce oven to 450 degrees and bake for 10 minutes longer. Combine egg and water. Remove tenderloin from oven and brush with egg and water mixture. Continue baking for 15 minutes for medium rare. Bake for an additional 15 minutes for medium. Serve on a platter and pass with Tarragon Hollandaise Sauce.

Tarragon Hollandaise Sauce

3 egg yolks
1 tablespoon water
1 teaspoon Dijon mustard
1½ tablespoons lemon juice
1 tablespoon tarragon vinegar

1 teaspoon dried tarragon leaves
Dash cayenne pepper
Dash white pepper
1 cup hot melted butter

Combine all ingredients except butter in a blender. Add butter gradually with motor running. Turn off when thick and serve.

Preparation Time: 1 hour 30 minutes

Cooking Time: 1 hour

Makes: 1¼ cups sauce

Serves: 6

Beef with Oyster Sauce

Oyster Sauce is a thick brown sauce made from oysters, soy sauce, and brine. Its rich flavor adds a smooth, somewhat salty taste to dishes for which there is no substitute.

1⅓ pounds beef fillet, thinly sliced
1½ tablespoons sake or red wine
2 teaspoons cornstarch
Salt
Freshly ground pepper
½ cup oil
3 cloves garlic, minced
3 tablespoons oyster sauce

2 tablespoons soy sauce
1 tablespoon lemon juice
1 tablespoon honey
3 thin slices fresh ginger
5 red chile peppers, fresh or dried, cut in half lengthwise
5 green onions, sliced diagonally into 1½-inch lengths

Cut beef into 1 × 1½-inch pieces. Marinate beef for 10 minutes in sake, cornstarch, salt, and pepper. Heat oil in a wok over high heat. Add garlic and stir fry until garlic is golden. Add oyster sauce, soy sauce, lemon juice, and honey. Add beef and stir fry for 30 seconds. Add ginger and stir fry for 3 minutes. Add chile peppers and green onions and stir fry for 1 minute.

Preparation Time: 45 minutes

Cooking Time: 10 minutes

Serves: 4

Oriental Flank Steak

½ cup soy sauce
3 tablespoons honey
1 teaspoon freshly grated ginger
1 clove garlic, crushed

3 tablespoons oil
2 tablespoons sesame seeds
½ cup chopped green onions
3 to 4 pounds flank steak

Combine soy sauce, honey, ginger, garlic, oil, sesame seeds, and green onions. Pour over flank steak and marinate for several hours or overnight in refrigerator. Grill steak to desired doneness. Slice across the grain.

Preparation Time: 15 minutes

Serves: 6 to 8

Note: Marinade goes equally well with grilled chicken and shrimp.

Southwestern Flank Steak with Fresh Fruit Salsa

Photograph appears with Table of Contents.

1½ pounds flank steak
¼ cup fresh orange juice
2 tablespoons chili sauce
2 tablespoons chili powder
2 tablespoons soy sauce
2 tablespoons oil
1 teaspoon honey
1 teaspoon grated orange peel
½ teaspoon grated lemon peel

2 cloves garlic, minced
½ teaspoon salt
¼ teaspoon cayenne pepper
1 medium orange, thinly sliced
Fresh Fruit Salsa to serve (recipe below)
Orange wedges for garnish
Cilantro sprigs for garnish

Place flank steak in a shallow baking dish. Combine orange juice, chili sauce, chili powder, soy sauce, oil, honey, orange peel, lemon peel, garlic, salt, and cayenne pepper. Pour over meat. Place orange slices over meat. Marinate in refrigerator overnight.

Preheat grill.

Bring meat to room temperature. Remove steak from marinade and discard marinade. Grill steak for 4 to 6 minutes per side or to desired doneness. Slice steak diagonally into thin slices. Place on a platter and surround with Fresh Fruit Salsa. Garnish with orange wedges and cilantro sprigs.

Fresh Fruit Salsa

1 cup diced pineapple
1 sliced kiwi
1 cup chopped papaya
½ teaspoon crushed hot red pepper flakes
½ cup diced red bell pepper

¼ cup diced green bell pepper
2½ tablespoons white wine vinegar
1½ tablespoons minced cilantro
4 teaspoons sugar

Combine ingredients in a bowl, mix well, and chill overnight. Serve at room temperature.

Preparation Time: 40 minutes (plus marinating overnight)

Cooking Time: 8 to 12 minutes

Serves: 4

Note: Great with grilled fish.

Grilled Sirloin Steak with Wine Sauce

Wine Suggestion:
Cabernet or Merlot

1 2 to 3-pound sirloin steak, 2-inches thick

3 cloves garlic, slivered

½ teaspoon salt

1 teaspoon freshly ground pepper

⅓ cup olive oil

1¼ teaspoons dried rosemary or 1 3-inch fresh sprig

¾ cup dry red wine

2 tablespoons butter

Preheat oven to 350 degrees.

Rub steak with 1 of the slivered cloves of garlic. Season with salt and pepper. Heat oil in a heavy skillet and brown steak on both sides to sear in juices, approximately 3 to 4 minutes on each side. Sprinkle with rosemary and place remaining slivered garlic on top. Place in a roasting pan. Put a meat thermometer in the center. Bake on upper rack for 25 to 30 minutes until thermometer reads 140 degrees for rare or for 35 minutes until thermometer reads 160 degrees for medium rare. Remove steak to a warmed platter. Skim fat from juices. Place roasting pan on stove over a medium-high flame. Add wine and boil. Whisk in butter. Pour 3 tablespoons sauce over steak. Slice. Serve with remaining wine sauce.

Preparation Time: 15 minutes

Cooking Time: 25 to 35 minutes

Serves: 6

Tornedos of Beef

Wine Suggestion:
Cabernet Sauvignon
or Merlot

5 tablespoons butter

4 slices French bread, ½ to ¾-inch thick

4 beef tenderloin fillets

2 cloves garlic, split

Salt

Freshly ground pepper

¾ cup sliced mushrooms

1 cup Madeira wine

2 tablespoons minced onion

1 cup consommé

1 tablespoon flour

Preheat oven to warm.

Melt 2 tablespoons butter in a heavy skillet. Sauté French bread until golden. Remove bread from pan and keep warm in oven. Rub fillets with garlic. Season with salt and pepper. Add 2 tablespoons butter to skillet. Sauté fillets to desired doneness (for medium rare, cook 3 minutes per side on medium-high heat and then 9 minutes per side on low heat). Remove fillets from pan and place on French bread and keep warm in oven. Add mushrooms to pan juices and sauté until tender. Add wine and simmer, scraping bottom of pan. Add onion and consommé. Bring to a low boil over a brisk flame for 3 minutes. Melt 1 tablespoon butter and blend in 1 tablespoon flour to make a paste. Add to wine mixture and simmer for 2 to 3 minutes. Season with freshly ground pepper. Remove fillets from oven and top with sauce.

Preparation Time: 45 minutes

Cooking Time: 25 minutes

Serves: 4

Note: An elegant and simple classic.

Moroccan Lamb with Poached Figs

Wine Suggestion:
Petite Sirah or
Zinfandel

Moroccan Lamb

2 tablespoons oil

2 tablespoons butter

1 onion, chopped

3 cloves garlic, minced

1 teaspoon ground ginger

¼ to ½ teaspoon cayenne pepper (amount based on preferred spiciness)

1 teaspoon ground tumeric

¼ teaspoon cinnamon

¼ teaspoon salt

1 teaspoon pepper

1 6-pound leg of lamb, butterflied, trimmed and cut into 1-inch cubes

16 ounces canned peeled tomatoes, chopped plus liquid

Water

1 cup raisins

2 tablespoons honey

Rice to serve

1 cup toasted slivered almonds to serve

Poached Figs to serve (recipe below)

Heat oil and butter in a large skillet. Sauté onion and garlic. Add ginger, cayenne pepper, tumeric, cinnamon, salt, pepper, and lamb. Brown lamb on all sides, stirring until cooked through. Add tomatoes, liquid from tomatoes, and enough water to cover half of the meat. Add raisins and honey. Bring to a boil and simmer until tender, about 30 to 40 minutes. Add more water if needed. Place in refrigerator overnight for best flavor. Reheat gently. Serve over rice. Top with toasted almonds and serve with Poached Figs.

Poached Figs

2 cups chicken broth

½ teaspoon ground ginger

¼ teaspoon cinnamon

¼ teaspoon salt

¼ teaspoon pepper

2 cups chopped dried figs or figlets cut in half

Heat broth in a saucepan with ginger, cinnamon, salt, and pepper. Bring to a boil. Add figs and simmer for 15 to 20 minutes until tender and soft.

Preparation Time: 1 hour

Cooking Time: 1 hour

Serves: 6

Note: The spicy sweet aroma of this exotic dish welcomes your guests. A perfect buffet choice.

Cinnamon Leg of Lamb

1 5 to 6-pound leg of lamb
3 cloves garlic, slivered
4 slices bacon
2 cups red wine
1 cup water
1 teaspoon dry mustard
1 onion, sliced

¼ teaspoon dried marjoram
¼ teaspoon dried sage
¼ teaspoon dried thyme
1 tablespoon Worcestershire sauce
1 beef bouillon cube
Cinnamon

Preheat oven to 350 degrees.

Place lamb in a roasting pan. Slit fat and insert slivers of garlic. Cover lamb with slices of bacon. Combine wine, water, mustard, onion, marjoram, sage, thyme, Worcestershire sauce, and bouillon cube. Stir until cube is dissolved. Pour over lamb. Shake cinnamon liberally over lamb. Roast for 2 hours or until meat thermometer registers 165 degrees (180 degrees for medium to well done). Baste every 20 minutes. Remove roast. Allow roast to rest for 5 minutes before carving.

Preparation Time: 15 minutes
Cooking Time: 2 hours
Serves: 6 to 8

Pork, Corn, and Tomato en Brochette with Hot Red Pepper Marinade

2 tablespoons red wine vinegar
1 tablespoon minced garlic
2 teaspoons crumbled dried oregano
1½ tablespoons hot red pepper flakes
1 shallot, minced
2 green onions, chopped
½ teaspoon salt

Freshly ground pepper
⅓ cup olive oil
1½ pounds pork tenderloin, trimmed and cubed
6 ears sweet corn
16 cherry tomatoes

Whisk together vinegar, garlic, oregano, red pepper flakes, shallot, green onions, salt, and pepper. Add oil in a stream, whisking until marinade is blended. Pour over pork and marinate in a shallow dish. Cover and chill for 4 hours.

Preheat grill.

Drain pork, reserving marinade. Chop each ear of corn into 4 pieces. Thread on skewers alternating pork, corn, and tomatoes. Grill brochettes for 25 minutes, basting and turning halfway through.

Preparation Time: 30 minutes

Cooking Time: 25 minutes

Serves: 6

Note: May be baked at 350 degrees for 1 hour.

Pork, Corn, and
Tomato en Brochette
with Hot Red Pepper
Marinade.

Calabasas Country Short Ribs

4 pounds short ribs, trimmed
1 onion, chopped
1 bay leaf
Salt
Pepper
Water
2 tablespoons oil
1 stalk celery, chopped
½ green bell pepper, seeded and
  chopped

1 clove garlic, minced
1 cup catsup
¼ tablespoon chili powder
1 teaspoon liquid smoke
½ teaspoon dried basil
½ teaspoon dried oregano
½ teaspoon ground cumin
¼ cup red wine vinegar

Combine ribs, half of the onion, bay leaf, salt, and pepper in a large pot. Cover with cold water and bring to a boil. Boil for 5 minutes. Skim and discard fat. Reduce heat, cover, and simmer until ribs are tender, approximately 1 hour to 1 hour 30 minutes. Drain ribs well, reserving 1 cup liquid. Heat oil in a saucepan over medium-low heat. Add remaining onion, celery, bell pepper, and garlic. Cook for 10 minutes or until tender, stirring occasionally. Add reserved cooking liquid and remaining ingredients and simmer for 30 minutes or until sauce is thick.

Preheat oven to 350 degrees.

Arrange ribs in a baking dish. Spoon sauce over ribs. Cover with foil and bake for 30 minutes.

Preparation Time: 45 minutes
Cooking Time: 2 hours
Serves: 4 to 6

Marinated Pork Kebabs

Wine Suggestion:
Light Zinfandel

¼ cup soy sauce
½ cup water
¼ cup honey
2 tablespoons red wine vinegar
1 tablespoon minced garlic
1 tablespoon freshly grated ginger
1 tablespoon chopped fresh cilantro
1 tablespoon paprika

Salt
Pepper
2½ pounds boneless pork loin, cut into 1½-inch cubes
¼ cup oil
1 tablespoon lemon juice
4 tablespoons butter

Combine soy sauce, water, honey, vinegar, garlic, ginger, cilantro, paprika, salt, and pepper. Pour mixture over pork and marinate for 24 hours in the refrigerator.

Pour marinade off pork and reserve in a separate bowl. Skewer pork cubes and brush with oil. Place skewers on grill and baste with marinade. Turn after 15 minutes. Baste with marinade and grill to desired doneness.

Combine ½ cup marinade, lemon juice, and butter in a saucepan. Heat well and serve with kebabs.

Preparation Time: 30 minutes
Cooking Time: 15 minutes
Serves: 4

Grilled Rosemary Porkchops

Rosemary is a distinctly flavored herb that according to folklore, "aids the memory".

1⅓ cups soy sauce
¾ cup water
¼ cup brown sugar

1 bunch fresh rosemary, chopped or ½ cup chopped dried rosemary
4 pork chops, extra thick

Combine soy sauce, water, sugar, and rosemary. Pour over pork chops. Marinate for 3 to 4 hours in refrigerator.

Preheat grill. Grill slowly over a low fire for 45 minutes or until done.

Preparation Time: 15 minutes plus 3 to 4 hours marinating time
Cooking Time: 45 minutes
Serves: 4

Tarragon Rabbit

Wine Suggestion:
Chardonnay or
Pinot Noir

2½ to 3½ pounds rabbit, cut up
½ cup fresh lemon juice
2 cups dry white wine
2 cloves garlic, minced
2 teaspoons crushed dried tarragon

½ cup butter
Salt
Pepper
½ cup light cream

Marinate rabbit pieces in lemon juice and wine. Refrigerate for at least 4 hours or overnight. Sauté garlic and tarragon in butter in a large skillet until garlic is golden. Remove garlic and discard. Add rabbit to skillet and reserve marinade. Brown rabbit on all sides. Add marinade, salt, and pepper. Bring to a boil. Reduce heat and simmer until tender. Remove rabbit. Stir cream into pan juices. Pour sauce over rabbit.

Preparation Time: 15 minutes
Cooking Time: 30 minutes
Serves: 4 to 6

Note: Rabbit is cooked when juices run clear after meat is pierced with a fork in the thickest part.

Ginger Stir Fry Spice

1-inch cube fresh ginger, peeled
2 large cloves garlic, peeled

1 small dried hot red pepper

Chop ingredients in a food processor. Store in an airtight container in the refrigerator.

Preparation Time: 15 minutes

Makes: Approximately 3 tablespoons

Note: This very hot and spicy seasoning is great with stir fry vegetables, chicken, shrimp, beef, and pork. Freezes well.

Mustard Dill Sauce

2 tablespoons prepared mustard
1 teaspoon dry mustard
¼ cup superfine sugar
¼ cup white vinegar

¾ cup oil
1 teaspoon dried dill
½ teaspoon salt

Whisk mustards, sugar, and vinegar together. Add oil in a stream gradually until well blended. Add dill and salt. Chill. Whisk again before serving.

Preparation Time: 15 minutes

Makes: Approximately 1½ cups

Note: Goes well with ham, fish, and melon.

Spicy Barbeque Sauce

1 lemon
2 tablespoons butter
¼ cup water
2 tablespoons Worcestershire sauce
1 clove garlic, crushed
4 tablespoons cider vinegar
1½ cups catsup
¼ teaspoon Tabasco sauce

3 tablespoons oil
¼ teaspoon red pepper flakes
2 tablespoons sugar
½ bay leaf
1 teaspoon paprika
Salt
Pepper

Quarter the lemon. Squeeze juice into a saucepan and add the lemon quarters. Combine remaining ingredients and heat thoroughly without boiling.

Preparation Time: 15 minutes

Cooking Time: 10 minutes

Makes: 2¾ cups

Note: Brush ribs or chicken with sauce while grilling.

Pacific Barbeque Sauce

1 cup soy sauce
1 tablespoon sugar
1 teaspoon dry mustard
1 teaspoon Tabasco sauce

2 cloves garlic, minced
1 small onion, grated
2 tablespoons bourbon
2 tablespoons minced fresh ginger

Combine ingredients. Marinate your choice of meat for several hours in the refrigerator, turning meat occasionally.

Preparation Time: 15 minutes

Makes: Approximately 2 cups

Note: Baste meat with sauce every 5 minutes when grilling.

Vegetables

Stir Fry Asparagus with Cashews

1½ pounds fresh asparagus
2 tablespoons olive oil
2 teaspoons sesame oil
2 teaspoons finely chopped fresh
　ginger

½ cup shitake mushrooms
½ cup whole roasted cashews
1 tablespoon soy sauce

Cut off the tough lower ends of asparagus spears and discard. Cut each spear diagonally into 2 or 3 pieces. Heat oils in a wok or skillet over high heat. Add ginger and stir fry for 1 minute. Add asparagus and stir fry for 2 minutes. Add mushrooms and stir fry until asparagus is tender but still crisp, approximately 3 minutes. Add cashews and soy sauce and toss.

Preparation Time:　15 minutes

Cooking Time:　10 minutes

Serves:　6

Note:　Should not be made ahead and cannot be frozen.

Asparagus with Caper Mayonnaise

1 cup mayonnaise
1 tablespoon capers
1 teaspoon caper juice
1 tablespoon anchovy paste
1 clove garlic, minced

⅛ teaspoon dried oregano leaves
1 tablespoon Dijon mustard
1 tablespoon fresh lemon juice
Dash white pepper
2 pounds asparagus

Blend all ingredients except asparagus in a food processor or blender until smooth. Cut off the tough lower ends of asparagus spears and discard. Steam asparagus until tender but still crisp (do not overcook). Place on individual plates and top with dressing.

Preparation Time:　10 minutes

Cooking Time:　Approximately 15 to 20 minutes

Serves:　4 to 6

Black Beans with Chorizo

1 pound black beans
Water
2 teaspoons salt
2 tablespoons olive oil
1 onion, chopped
2 cloves garlic, minced
4 pickled jalapeño peppers, seeded
   and finely chopped
1 teaspoon ground marjoram
1 teaspoon ground oregano

1 teaspoon ground cumin
Salt
Pepper
1 cup tomato juice
½ pound chorizo
Chopped onions to serve
Chopped tomatoes to serve
Chopped cilantro to serve
Shredded Cheddar cheese to serve
Sour cream to serve

Rinse beans. Place in a large pot and cover with water. Add salt and cook over low heat, maintaining water level so that the beans do not stick. Cook for at least 4 hours or until beans are very tender and mixture is thick.

Heat oil in a skillet over medium heat. Add onion and garlic. Sauté until transparent. Add peppers, marjoram, oregano, cumin, salt, pepper, and tomato juice. Simmer for 20 minutes. Add 2 cups of beans to sauce and mash well. Add mixture to the pot of beans. Discard casing on chorizo, if any. Fry chorizo in a skillet until browned. Add to the beans and cook for 20 minutes more. Serve with chopped onions, tomatoes, cilantro, Cheddar cheese, and sour cream.

Preparation Time: 30 minutes
Cooking Time: 4 hours 40 minutes
Serves: 6 to 8

Note: A great variation to the traditional refried beans.

Green Beans with Orange Sauce

2 teaspoons butter
1 teaspoon olive oil
¼ cup chopped green onions
1 clove garlic, minced
½ cup freshly squeezed orange juice

¼ cup dry white wine
2 quarts water, salted
1¼ pounds green beans, trimmed and cut in half lengthwise
1 tablespoon grated orange peel

Heat butter and olive oil in a small saucepan over low heat. Add green onions and garlic and sauté until soft, about 3 to 4 minutes. Add orange juice and wine. Increase heat to high and boil until thick and syrup-like, about 4 minutes, stirring often. Set aside.

Bring water to a rapid boil over high heat. Add green beans and cook until tender but crisp, about 4 to 5 minutes. Drain well and pat dry. Transfer beans to a serving dish. Add sauce and toss gently. Sprinkle with orange peel.

Preparation Time: 20 minutes

Cooking Time: 20 minutes

Serves: 4 to 6

Note: Prepare just before serving. An elegant way to dress up an old favorite.

Ruby Carrots

2 pounds carrots, peeled and cut into 1½-inch pieces
1½ cups halved seedless red grapes

¼ cup honey
2 tablespoons butter
⅛ teaspoon ground ginger (optional)

Preheat oven to 250 degrees.

Steam carrots until tender. Combine carrots with other ingredients in a covered casserole. Warm in oven for 15 minutes.

Preparation Time: 15 minutes

Cooking Time: 15 minutes

Serves: 10

California Corn Pudding

¼ cup butter	3 eggs, beaten until frothy
¼ cup flour	1 tablespoon dried marjoram leaves
1 teaspoon salt	1 teaspoon freshly grated nutmeg
1½ tablespoons sugar	5 slices Cheddar cheese
1⅓ cups milk	2 slices bacon
3 cups corn (fresh or frozen)	

Preheat oven to 350 degrees.

Melt butter in a saucepan. Stir in flour, salt, and sugar. Cook until bubbly. Add milk and cook until thick, stirring occasionally. Stir in corn, eggs, marjoram, and nutmeg. Pour into a well buttered 2-quart casserole. Top with slices of cheese. Cook bacon until done, but not crisp. Slice into 1-inch pieces and lay on top of pudding. Place casserole in a hot water bath and bake for 45 to 50 minutes.

Preparation Time: 20 minutes

Cooking Time: 45 to 50 minutes

Serves: 6

Honey Carrots Purée

8 carrots	¼ teaspoon ground nutmeg
3 tablespoons butter	⅛ teaspoon ground ginger
½ teaspoon cinnamon	2¼ tablespoons honey

Peel carrots and slice in half. Steam for 20 minutes or until tender. Drain well. Purée in a food processor, with metal blade, for 30 seconds. Scrape sides. Add butter and purée for 30 seconds. Add spices and, with motor running, add honey. Purée for 1 minute or until smooth. Reheat, if necessary.

Preparation Time: 10 minutes

Cooking Time: 20 minutes

Serves: 4

Note: May pipe out in florets using a star-tipped pastry bag.

Cauliflower with Mushroom Sauce

3 cups cauliflowerets, cooked until
    tender
3 tablespoons butter
1 cup sliced mushrooms
2 tablespoons chopped green onions
2 tablespoons flour

Salt
White pepper
¾ cup heavy cream
¼ cup freshly grated Parmesan
    cheese

Preheat oven to 450 degrees.

Arrange cauliflowerets in a small baking dish. Set aside. Melt butter in a skillet.
Add mushrooms and green onions. Sauté for 1 minute. Stir in flour, salt, and
pepper. Sauté, stirring constantly, until flour is absorbed. Pour in cream. Cook
until slightly thickened. Pour sauce over cauliflower and sprinkle top with
Parmesan cheese. Bake for 10 to 15 minutes or until top is golden.

Preparation Time: 10 minutes
Cooking Time: 10 to 15 minutes
Serves: 4

Snow Peas and Three Mushrooms

2 tablespoons oil
¾ pound snow peas, trimmed
10 mushrooms, sliced
½ cup hydrated or fresh sliced oyster
    mushrooms

½ cup hydrated or fresh sliced wood
    ear mushrooms
¼ cup soy sauce
1 tablespoon plus 1 teaspoon oyster
    sauce

Heat oil in a skillet or wok. Sauté snow peas for about 3 minutes. Add mushrooms, soy sauce, and oyster sauce. Stir fry for about 5 minutes or until snow
peas are tender but crisp.

Preparation Time: 10 minutes
Cooking Time: 8 to 10 minutes
Serves: 4 to 6

Note: If using dried mushrooms, soak in warm water to cover for 30 minutes to
hydrate.

Spicy Cauliflower Sauté

3 tablespoons oil

1 head cauliflower, broken into florets
and thinly sliced

1 2-inch piece ginger, peeled and very
thinly sliced

1 clove garlic, minced

½ teaspoon ground tumeric

4 fresh plum tomatoes, peeled,
seeded, and chopped

3 tablespoons dry white wine

¼ cup water

4 green onions plus tops, chopped

¼ teaspoon white pepper

Salt

Heat oil over moderately high heat in a large skillet until hot, but not smoking. Sauté the cauliflower for 3 minutes or until golden, stirring once. Add ginger, garlic, and tumeric. Sauté mixture, stirring for 30 seconds. Add tomatoes, wine, and water. Bring to a boil. Simmer for 8 to 10 minutes or until the cauliflower is just tender. Stir in green onions, pepper, and salt.

Preparation Time: 15 minutes

Cooking Time: 15 minutes

Serves: 2 to 4

Note: Best if prepared just prior to serving.

Artichoke Vegetable Melange

Dressing
1 cup mayonnaise

1 cup plain yogurt

1 clove garlic, crushed

1 tablespoon chopped fresh parsley

1 teaspoon dried basil

1 teaspoon chopped onion

¼ teaspoon salt

3 teaspoons dried thyme

Combine dressing ingredients and chill.

Artichoke Vegetable Melange
2 tablespoons oil

¼ cup chopped onion

¾ cup pearl onions

1 clove garlic, crushed

¾ cup sliced zucchini

½ cup diced green bell pepper

¼ teaspoon salt

¼ teaspoon pepper

7¼ ounce can small whole carrots

¾ cup cubed tomatoes

4 cooked artichokes

Heat oil in a large skillet. Add onions and garlic. Sauté onions until tender, approximately 2 minutes. Add zucchini, bell pepper, salt, and pepper. Sauté for 2 minutes more. Remove from heat. Add carrots and tomatoes. Cover and chill.

Pull out centers of artichokes gently. Scoop out all "choke" until clean. Spoon vegetables into artichokes. Chill. Serve artichokes with dressing on the side.

Preparation Time: 25 minutes

Cooking Time: 45 minutes for artichokes, 5 minutes for vegetables

Serves: 4

Artichoke Vegetable
Melange.

Beets Purée with Cilantro

3 to 4 medium beets, ends trimmed
3 tablespoons butter, softened
7 tablespoons sour cream, divided
1 orange

4 teaspoons chopped fresh cilantro
½ teaspoon salt
¼ teaspoon white pepper
Cilantro sprigs for garnish

Cook beets in boiling water for 40 minutes or until tender. Drain and cool slightly. Peel and dice. Chop beets with butter and 3 tablespoons sour cream in a food processor or blender until smooth in texture. Cut orange in half. Juice 1 half and remove orange segments from remaining half. Reserve segments. Add orange juice, cilantro, salt, and pepper to beets and blend well. Transfer to a saucepan and reheat over low heat. Garnish each serving with 1 tablespoon sour cream, 1 orange segment, and cilantro sprigs.

Preparation Time: 15 minutes

Cooking Time: 50 minutes

Serves: 4

Note: Beets may be cooked in advance and stored overnight. Reheat beets before blending.

Bel Air Honey Broccoli

1½ pounds broccoli, cut into florets
2½ tablespoons sesame oil
2 tablespoons honey
2 tablespoons soy sauce

¼ pound snow peas
4 ounces enoki mushrooms
½ cup sesame seeds, toasted

Steam broccoli until tender but crisp, about 4 minutes. Drain and set aside.

Heat sesame oil, honey, and soy sauce in a small saucepan and stir until well mixed. Stir in snow peas and sauté for 3 minutes. Add enoki mushrooms and cook for an additional minute. Pour over hot broccoli and toss with sesame seeds.

Preparation Time: 10 minutes

Cooking Time: 15 minutes

Serves: 4 to 6

Broccoli Rabe with Lemon and Garlic

Rabe is sometimes called Rapini. Broccoli rabe "behaves" like spinach while cooking. If unable to locate broccoli rabe, florets of broccoli may be substituted.

1½ pounds pencil-thin broccoli rabe, washed
Water
2½ teaspoons minced garlic
3 tablespoons butter
3 tablespoons minced fresh parsley

Salt
Pepper
2½ teaspoons freshly grated lemon rind

Discard any yellow leaves and course stems of rabe. Cook the rabe in water in a covered heavy pan over moderately high heat, stirring occasionally, until stems are just tender. Sauté garlic in butter over moderately low heat for 3 minutes, stirring occasionally. Drain the broccoli rabe, transfer it to a bowl, and pour the garlic mixture over it. Add parsley, salt, and pepper and toss mixture gently until it is combined well. Sprinkle with lemon rind.

Preparation Time: 10 minutes

Cooking Time: 7 minutes

Serves: 4

Broccoli with Olive Nut Sauce

½ cup butter
½ cup slivered almonds, lightly toasted
3 tablespoons fresh lemon juice

1 clove garlic, crushed
⅔ cup ripe olives, rinsed and sliced
White pepper
3 pounds fresh broccoli, trimmed

Melt butter in a small skillet. Add almonds, lemon juice, garlic, olives, and pepper. Sauté until heated through. Allow mixture to stand for 1 hour.

Steam broccoli until tender. Reheat sauce. Place broccoli in a serving dish and pour warm sauce over.

Preparation Time: 1 hour 15 minutes (including standing time)

Cooking Time: 10 minutes

Serves: 8

Note: Sauce may be made the night before and reheated, but do not freeze.

Calabacitas

3 cloves garlic
2 Anaheim chiles
1 cup chopped onion
3 green onions, chopped
¾ pound zucchini
1 red bell pepper
4 tablespoons butter
2 tablespoons oil

2 cups fresh corn
Salt
Pepper
1 teaspoon ground cumin
⅓ cup heavy cream
⅓ cup shredded Cheddar cheese
⅓ cup shredded Monterey jack cheese

Mince garlic, chiles, and onions in a food processor, adding each item 1 at a time while motor is running. Coarsely chop zucchini and bell pepper by hand. Heat butter and oil in a large skillet. Add the garlic, chile, and onion mixture and sauté over medium heat for about 3 minutes, stirring occasionally. Add zucchini and bell pepper and sauté until tender, about 5 minutes. Add corn, salt, pepper, cumin, and cream and stir gently. Cover and cook over low heat for about 5 minutes. Add cheeses just before serving, allowing cheeses to melt slightly.

Preparation Time: 30 minutes

Cooking Time: 15 to 20 minutes

Serves: 4 to 6

Note: This dish goes well with flour tortillas and refried beans.

Corn and Jalapeño Pepper Soufflé

4 tablespoons unsalted butter

2 tablespoons dry bread crumbs

½ red onion, minced

3 tablespoons flour

1 cup milk

3 egg yolks

2 fresh jalapeño peppers, seeded and minced

1½ cups fresh blanched corn (or thawed, frozen corn)

1 cup shredded mild Cheddar cheese

2 teaspoons plus pinch salt

¼ teaspoon white pepper

5 egg whites, room temperature

¼ teaspoon cream of tartar

Preheat oven to 375 degrees. Coat bottom and sides of a 1½-quart soufflé dish with 1 tablespoon butter and bread crumbs. Place in refrigerator.

Sauté onion in 3 tablespoons butter in a heavy saucepan over moderately low heat. Add flour and cook, stirring for 3 minutes. Add milk slowly while whisking and bring to a boil. Beat in egg yolks. Stir in peppers, corn, cheese, 2 teaspoons salt, and pepper.

Beat egg whites with a pinch of salt in a large bowl until frothy. Add cream of tartar and beat until whites hold stiff peaks. Stir ¼ of the whites into corn mixture. Fold corn and whites mixture very gently into the remaining whites. Spoon mixture gently into prepared dish. Bake for 20 to 25 minutes or until top is golden (the center will be moist).

Preparation Time: 30 minutes

Cooking Time: 20 to 25 minutes

Serves: 6

Sierra Spinach

4 bunches fresh spinach (or 2 10-ounce frozen packages)
½ cup butter, softened
¾ cup fine dry bread crumbs
2 green onions, finely chopped
1 teaspoon minced garlic
½ teaspoon pepper
Salt

2 eggs, beaten
Pinch thyme
1½ teaspoons Tabasco sauce
¼ cup freshly grated Parmesan cheese
5 to 6 tomatoes, cut in ½-inch thick slices

Preheat oven to 350 degrees.

Cook spinach and drain well. Chop coarsely. Combine with all remaining ingredients except tomatoes and blend well. Place in a baking dish and bake for 15 minutes. Put tomato slices on a baking sheet. Place in oven and bake both for 10 minutes longer. Place a rounded spoonful or an ice cream scoop of spinach mixture on top of each tomato slice to serve.

Preparation Time: 15 minutes
Cooking Time: 25 minutes
Serves: 5 to 6

Note: The spinach mixture can be prepared in advance and refrigerated until ready to bake.

Spinach Roulade with Mushroom Filling

10 ounces frozen chopped spinach,
  cooked and well drained
2 egg yolks
¼ cup minced onion
2½ teaspoons butter
Freshly ground nutmeg

Freshly ground pepper
4 egg whites
⅓ cup freshly grated Parmesan
  cheese
½ pound mushrooms, sliced
½ cup Neufchâtel cheese

Preheat oven to 375 degrees.

Combine cooked spinach and egg yolks in a bowl. Sauté onion in 1 teaspoon butter until tender. Add to spinach. Season with nutmeg and pepper. Set aside. Beat egg whites until they form soft peaks. Stir a third of the egg whites into the spinach mixture, then fold in remaining whites.

Line a baking sheet with buttered parchment or foil. Spread spinach mixture on paper to make a 12 × 18-inch rectangle. Sprinkle with Parmesan cheese and bake for 10 to 12 minutes. Sauté mushrooms in 1½ teaspoons butter until tender. Remove from heat and stir in Neufchâtel cheese. Set aside. Turn out roulade onto a towel or foil. Spread mushroom mixture gently and evenly over roulade, leaving a ½-inch border. Roll up very gently. Transfer roll carefully to a serving platter. Slice to serve.

Preparation Time: 20 minutes
Cooking Time: 12 minutes
Serves: 4 to 6

Note: Must be made and served immediately. Rolling the roulade *very carefully* is essential to ensure a lovely presentation.

Herbed Melonseed Pasta

½ pound melonseed pasta
5 cloves garlic
½ cup fresh basil leaves, lightly packed
½ cup fresh parsley, lighted packed
2 tablespoons fresh thyme leaves
2 tablespoons fresh oregano leaves

¼ cup freshly grated Parmesan cheese
½ cup olive oil
¼ cup white wine vinegar
Salt
Pepper
1 ripe but firm tomato, chopped

Cook pasta according to package directions. Purée garlic, basil, parsley, thyme, oregano, and Parmesan cheese in a food processor until coarse. Add olive oil in a steady stream while motor is running. Add vinegar, salt, and pepper. Toss hot pasta with herb purée. Add the chopped tomato and toss lightly.

Preparation Time: 20 minutes

Cooking Time: 10 minutes (according to package directions for pasta)

Serves: 4 to 6

Note: Melonseed pasta is sometimes called semi de melone, Rosamaria, or Orzo.

Caponata
(Italian Eggplant)

1 red bell pepper, chunked
1 yellow bell pepper, chunked
1 green bell pepper, chunked
½ cup light olive oil
1 whole eggplant, cubed
1½ onions, chopped
2 cloves garlic, chopped

1 teaspoon salt
1 teaspoon pepper
10 fresh basil leaves, finely chopped
1 cup tomato sauce
¼ cup freshly grated Parmesan cheese

Preheat oven to 375 degrees.

Sauté bell peppers in olive oil until tender. Add eggplant, onions, garlic, salt, pepper, and basil. Sauté until eggplant is cooked, about 10 minutes. Transfer to a shallow baking dish and cover with tomato sauce. Sprinkle with Parmesan cheese. Bake for 20 minutes.

Preparation Time: 30 minutes

Cooking Time: 20 minutes

Serves: 6

Risotto with Asparagus and Pine Nuts

1 pound fresh asparagus
1 shallot, minced
2 tablespoons butter
½ pound uncooked rice (risotto or any long rice)
½ cup dry white wine
2 to 3 cups chicken broth

6 tablespoons freshly grated Parmesan cheese
¾ cup heavy cream
Salt
½ teaspoon pepper
2 cloves garlic, minced
½ cup pine nuts, toasted

Cut off asparagus tips and set aside. Cut stems into thin rounds and set aside. Sauté shallot in butter until golden. Stir in rice. Add wine and cook, stirring continuously, until wine evaporates. Add asparagus stems. Stir in broth gradually, ½ cup at a time, as rice absorbs broth. Continue stirring until rice is tender. Add Parmesan cheese, cream, salt, pepper, and garlic. Add asparagus tips and pine nuts just before serving and allow to rest for 5 minutes.

Preparation Time: 20 minutes
Cooking Time: Approximately 45 minutes
Serves: 6 to 8

Note: Risotto is the preferred rice for this dish. It can be found in specialty markets. Japanese rice would be a great alternative.

Tabule

1½ cups cracked wheat bulgar
Hot water
1 pint cherry tomatoes, quartered
1 bunch green onions, chopped
1 cucumber, peeled and chopped
1 green bell pepper, chopped
1 large bunch fresh parsley, finely
   chopped

3 lemons, juiced
½ cup oil
1 teaspoon cinnamon
1½ teaspoons chopped fresh mint
1 tablespoon salt
1 teaspoon finely ground pepper

Soak cracked wheat in a bowl of water to cover for 35 to 45 minutes. Drain well. Add chopped vegetables and parsley. Set aside. Combine lemon juice, oil, cinnamon, mint, salt, and pepper. Mix well and pour over vegetables. Toss well. Cover and refrigerate for at least 4 hours or overnight.

Preparation Time: 45 minutes (about 15 minutes if using food processor)
Serves: 8

Note: May substitute 3 large seeded tomatoes instead of cherry tomatoes. Will keep in refrigerator for several days if covered tightly. Excellent when stuffed in a pita or served with crisp whole grain crackers.

Red Potatoes with Prosciutto and Chives

²/₃ pound thinly sliced prosciutto
2 cloves garlic, minced
2 pounds small red potatoes, quartered
Water
Salt

¼ cup butter, cut into small pieces and softened
½ cup chicken broth
1 tablespoon red or white vinegar
¼ cup chopped fresh chives
Pepper

Cut proscuitto into small pieces. Sauté prosciutto and garlic for 4 to 5 minutes over medium heat. Drain on paper towels and set aside. Place potatoes in a large saucepan. Add enough cold salted water to cover by at least 2-inches. Bring to a boil and simmer potatoes until just tender, about 8 to 12 minutes. Drain. Transfer to a bowl and toss gently with butter, broth, and vinegar. Add prosciutto, garlic, chives, and pepper. Toss to combine. Transfer to a serving dish.

Preparation Time: 15 minutes

Cooking Time: 20 minutes

Serves: 6

Yams with Maple Pecan Butter

6 to 8 medium yams, scrubbed and pierced
½ cup butter, softened
⅓ cup maple syrup

⅛ teaspoon ground mace
¼ teaspoon salt
3 tablespoons diced pecans

Preheat oven to 400 degrees.

Bake yams in glass baking dish until tender, about 45 minutes. Cream butter until fluffy. Beat in maple syrup gradually. Stir in mace, salt, and pecans. Score with an X-shape cut across the tops of the baked yams. Press open and top each with 1 tablespoon of maple pecan butter and serve.

Preparation Time: 15 minutes

Cooking Time: 45 minutes

Serves: 6 to 8

Note: Topping may be doubled for those who wish a more flavorful yam.

Red Potatoes with Prosciutto and Chives; Tomatoes with Dill Sauce.

257 Vegetables

Herbed Spaghetti Squash

4 pounds spaghetti squash
1 onion, chopped
¼ cup diced bell pepper
1 tablespoon olive oil
1 can sliced black olives
1 clove garlic, minced

1 to 2 teaspoons herbs of Provence
1 teaspoon salt
Pepper
3 tablespoons butter
2 cups shredded Monterey jack cheese

Preheat oven to 350 degrees.

Pierce squash deeply with a knife 3 to 4 times. Bake for 45 minutes. Cut squash in half. Scoop out seeds and discard. Remove strands of squash with a fork. Set aside. Discard shells. Sauté onion and bell pepper in olive oil until tender. Add squash and toss well. Add olives, garlic, and seasonings and mix well. Place in a 1½-quart baking dish. Dot with butter and sprinkle with cheese. Bake uncovered for 10 to 15 minutes.

Preparation Time: 30 minutes
Cooking Time: 15 minutes
Serves: 6

Note: Squash can be microwaved on high for 20 minutes, turning after 10 minutes. Casserole may be microwaved on high for 2 to 3 minutes until cheese melts. May substitute 1 cup jalapeño cheese for 1 cup Monterey jack cheese. May add 1 medium tomato, chopped, to be sautéed with onion and bell pepper.

Butternut Squash Purée

2¾ pounds butternut squash
Water
½ cup butter, softened and cut into
   small pieces
2 tablespoons dark brown sugar,
   packed

½ teaspoon freshly grated orange rind
¼ teaspoon freshly grated nutmeg
Pepper
Cinnamon for garnish

Cook squash in a pot of boiling water for 20 minutes or until tender. Drain well. Peel, seed, and cube.

Preheat oven to 350 degrees.

Beat squash until smooth with an electric mixer. Beat in butter, brown sugar, orange rind, nutmeg, and pepper. Transfer squash to a well buttered 1-quart baking dish. Sprinkle with cinnamon, if desired. Cover dish and bake for 35 to 45 minutes or until bubbly.

Preparation Time: 30 minutes

Cooking Time: 45 minutes

Serves: 6

Note: For individual servings, serve in hollowed out orange shell halves.

Tomatoes with Dill Sauce

½ cup sour cream
¼ cup mayonnaise
2 tablespoons grated onion
¼ teaspoon dried dill

¼ teaspoon salt
¼ teaspoon white pepper
4 large tomatoes
Dill sprigs for garnish

Combine sour cream, mayonnaise, onion, dill, salt, and pepper. Mix well. Peel tomatoes. Core and cut in half. Place in an ovenproof serving dish. Broil tomatoes for 2 to 3 minutes or until hot. Spoon mixture over hot tomatoes. Garnish with dill sprigs.

Preparation Time: 15 minutes

Cooking Time: 3 minutes

Serves: 4

Acorn Squash Soufflé

3 tablespoons butter
3 tablespoons flour
1 cup boiling milk
4 egg yolks

2 acorn squash
3 tablespoons brown sugar
5 egg whites

Melt butter in a saucepan. Stir in flour and blend. Add boiling milk and stir over medium heat until consistency is thick and smooth. Add egg yolks, 1 at a time, stirring well after each addition. Set aside. Pierce squash and cook in microwave on high for 10 minutes. Remove from microwave. Cut open and remove seeds. Return to microwave and cook on high until tender, approximately 10 minutes more. Remove squash from shell. Mash squash and measure out ¾ cup. Blend with brown sugar until smooth. Mix in hot milk sauce.

Preheat oven to 350 degrees.

Whip egg whites until stiff peaks form. Fold into squash mixture. Turn into 1½-quart soufflé dish. Bake for 30 to 40 minutes.

Preparation Time: 30 minutes
Cooking Time: 30 to 40 minutes
Serves: 4

Note: Squash may be steamed until tender, about 20 to 25 minutes.

Zucchini with Pesto Sauce

2 cups fresh basil
½ cup olive oil
1 tablespoon chopped fresh parsley
2 cloves garlic
1 teaspoon salt
⅛ teaspoon pepper

4 tablespoons pine nuts
2 tablespoons butter
6 small zucchini, quartered
1 cup freshly grated Parmesan cheese
⅛ cup pine nuts

Chop basil until fine in a food processor, about 3 seconds. Add oil, parsley, garlic, salt, pepper, and pine nuts. Purée mixture. Set aside.

Melt butter in a medium skillet. Sauté zucchini until tender but firm. Add pesto sauce and warm over low heat. Remove to serving dish and sprinkle with Parmesan cheese and pine nuts.

Preparation Time: 15 minutes

Cooking Time: 10 minutes

Serves: 4

Note: Pesto sauce may be made ahead. Entire dish, however, should be prepared just prior to serving.

Minted Zucchini

2 pounds zucchini
2 tablespoons olive oil
1 tablespoon butter
1 teaspoon salt

½ teaspoon pepper
½ cup chopped fresh mint
¼ teaspoon sugar
Fresh mint sprigs for garnish

Cut zucchini into eighths lengthwise to form sticks. Cut sticks in half crosswise. Heat oil and butter in a large skillet or wok. Add zucchini, tossing constantly for 3 to 5 minutes. Add salt, pepper, mint, and sugar. Sauté for 3 to 5 minutes more (do not overcook). Garnish with fresh mint sprigs.

Preparation Time: 10 minutes

Cooking Time: 6 to 10

Serves: 4

Bulgar Pilaf with Cashews

1 small onion, thinly sliced
1½ tablespoons butter
½ cups cracked wheat bulgar
¾ cup chicken broth

Freshly ground pepper
3 tablespoons whole roasted cashews
1½ tablespoons sliced green onions

Sauté onion in butter in a small saucepan over moderately low heat, stirring until onion is tender. Stir in bulgar and cook, stirring for 1 minute. Add broth and bring to a boil. Cover and cook mixture over low heat for 10 minutes or until the liquid is absorbed. Fluff the mixture with a fork. Transfer to a serving dish. Season with pepper. Top with cashews and green onions.

Preparation Time: 15 minutes

Cooking Time: 15 minutes

Serves: 4 to 6

Note: May be made in advance. However, do not top with nuts and green onions until ready to serve. Some broth may need to be added when reheating.

Rice Pilaf

½ cup butter
1 onion, chopped
21 ounces beef consommé
1 cup white rice
¼ cup cracked wheat bulgar

1 cup sliced mushrooms
1½ tablespoons pine nuts
1 tablespoon finely chopped fresh parsley

Heat butter in a medium skillet. Add onion and sauté for 2 minutes. Blend in remaining ingredients. Cover and simmer over low heat for 25 to 30 minutes.

Preparation Time: 5 minutes

Cooking Time: 30 minutes

Serves: 4 to 6

Hacienda Rice

½ cup butter
1 onion, chopped
3 cloves garlic, minced
4 cups freshly cooked white rice
2 cups sour cream
1 cup cottage cheese
1 tablespoon Worcestershire sauce
1 teaspoon beau monde

2 bay leaves, crumbled
½ teaspoon salt
¼ teaspoon pepper
1½ cups shredded Cheddar cheese
1½ cups shredded Monterey jack cheese
8 ounces diced green chiles
2 zucchini, grated and patted very dry
Chopped fresh parsley for garnish

Preheat oven to 375 degrees.

Melt butter in a large skillet. Sauté onion and garlic until tender. Add cooked rice, sour cream, cottage cheese, Worcestershire sauce, beau monde, bay leaves, salt, and pepper. Mix well. Oil a 4-quart casserole. Combine cheeses. Divide the rice mixture into thirds. Spread a third of the rice mixture, then half of the chiles, half of the zucchini, and 1 cup of the combined cheeses into the prepared casserole. Repeat layers ending with the last third of rice mixture. Top with remaining 1 cup of combined cheeses. Bake uncovered for 25 to 30 minutes or until bubbly. Sprinkle with chopped parsley.

Preparation Time: 45 minutes
Cooking Time: 50 minutes (includes time for cooking rice)
Serves: 8

Note: This is a unique alternative to the traditional Mexican rice.

Desserts

Lemon Cream in Meringue Shell

When beating egg whites, always use a clean, dry glass or metal (preferably copper) bowl to achieve maximum volume.

Meringue Shell

4 egg whites

1 teaspoon cream of tartar

1 cup sugar

Preheat oven to 300 degrees. Butter a 9-inch pie plate generously.

Beat egg whites until frothy. Add cream of tartar and beat until soft peaks form. Add sugar gradually and beat until very stiff. Spoon meringue into the prepared pie plate, making edges higher to form a pie shell. Bake for 35 to 40 minutes. Set aside to cool thoroughly.

Filling

4 egg yolks

½ cup sugar

3 tablespoons lemon juice

2 teaspoons lemon zest

1 cup heavy cream

Lightly beat egg yolks. Pour into top of double boiler. Add sugar, lemon juice, and zest and blend thoroughly. Cook, stirring occasionally, over hot water for 15 to 20 minutes or until mixture becomes thick. Allow to cool thoroughly. Whip the cream in a separate bowl until stiff peaks form. Add 2 tablespoons whipped cream to the now cooled lemon-egg mixture. Blend to lighten. Fold the lemon-egg mixture gently into the whipped cream. Spoon filling into the meringue shell, leaving a meringue crust edge.

Chill thoroughly before serving. Best if served the day it is made. Meringue will soften overnight.

Preparation Time: 40 minutes

Cooking Time: 1 hour

Serves: 8

Lemon Curd and Kiwi Tartlets

Tartlets

½ cup unsalted butter, softened

⅓ cup sugar

¾ cup flour

½ cup rolled oats

¼ teaspoon salt

Preheat oven to 350 degrees. Butter mini-muffin cups.

Cream butter and sugar until mixture is light and fluffy. Add flour, oats, and salt. Blend mixture until just combined (do not overwork). Press 1 rounded teaspoon of dough into the bottom and all the way up the sides of each prepared cup. Chill shells for 15 minutes.

Bake for 10 to 12 minutes or until golden around the edges. Allow to cool in muffin pan for 5 minutes, then loosen with the tip of a sharp knife and transfer to a rack to cool completely.

Lemon Curd

2 eggs

½ cup unsalted butter, cut into bits

½ cup sugar

1½ tablespoons freshly grated lemon zest

¼ cup fresh lemon juice

2 kiwis, peeled, sliced, and quartered for garnish

Combine eggs, butter, sugar, lemon zest, and lemon juice in a saucepan. Cook mixture over medium heat, whisking constantly, until curd is thick enough to hold the mark of the whisk and the first bubbles appear on the surface. Transfer curd to a bowl. Allow to cool. Cover with a buttered round of wax paper and chill for 1 hour.

Fill each tartlet with a mound of lemon curd. Top with kiwi.

Preparation Time: 30 minutes plus 1 hour 20 minutes chilling time

Cooking Time: 15 minutes

Makes: 35

Note: Shells may be made 2 days in advance and kept in an airtight container or frozen indefinitely. Curd may be made 2 days in advance, kept covered, and chilled. Assemble just before serving. Tartlets may be filled with fresh fruit and whipped cream for variation.

Chilled Lime Soufflé with Strawberry Sauce

Soufflé
1½ teaspoons unflavored gelatin
¾ cup lime juice
1 cup sugar
6 eggs, separated
2 tablespoons unsalted butter

½ teaspoon vanilla
Zest of 1 lime
Strawberry Sauce to serve (recipe below)
Fresh berries for garnish

Combine gelatin and ¼ cup lime juice. Allow to soften. Set aside.

Whisk ½ cup sugar, egg yolks, and remaining ½ cup lime juice in a large saucepan. Whisk over low heat until mixture thickens slightly. Remove from heat and continue stirring. Add butter, softened gelatin, vanilla, and lime zest. Whisk until thoroughly blended. Chill for 30 minutes. Beat egg whites. Add remaining sugar gradually when whites start to form stiff peaks. Beat until sugar is dissolved and peaks are thick and shiny. Add a little of the egg whites to the lime mixture to lighten it. Fold in remaining egg whites gently. Turn mixture into a soufflé dish and gently cover with plastic wrap. Refrigerate for at least 4 hours or overnight. Serve with Strawberry Sauce and garnish with fresh berries.

Strawberry Sauce
3 cups fresh strawberries, hulled
¼ cup sugar
Dash lemon juice

2 tablespoons Chambord (raspberry liqueur)

Place strawberries in a food processor or blender and purée. Add sugar, lemon juice, and liqueur. Blend until sugar is dissolved, about 1½ to 2 minutes.

Preparation Time: 1 hour 10 minutes

Serves: 8

Chilled Lime Soufflé with Strawberry Sauce.

Note: Make Strawberry Sauce only a few hours before serving and always keep refrigerated. It does not keep. Strawberry Sauce makes an excellent base for strawberry ice cream.

Chocolate Peppermint Torte

Crust
1 cup chocolate wafer crumbs
2 tablespoons butter, melted

Preheat oven to 350 degrees.

Combine chocolate wafer crumbs and butter. Press into the bottom and up the sides of a 9-inch springform pan. Bake for 7 minutes. Set aside to cool.

Filling
½ cup butter, softened
¾ cup sugar
4 ounces unsweetened baking chocolate
1 teaspoon vanilla

½ teaspoon peppermint extract
3 eggs
½ cup heavy cream, whipped
Fresh mint leaves for garnish

Cream butter, adding sugar gradually, until light and fluffy. Melt 3 ounces chocolate in a separate pan. Beat melted chocolate, vanilla, and peppermint extract into butter mixture. Add eggs, 1 at a time, beating well after each addition. Fold in the whipped cream. Spoon filling into crust. Grate 1 ounce chocolate and sprinkle over filling. Cover tightly with plastic wrap and refrigerate for 4 hours. Garnish with mint leaves.

Preparation Time: 30 minutes
Cooking Time: 7 minutes
Serves: 6 to 8

Chocolate Soufflé pour Deux

2 tablespoons butter
4 teaspoons flour
¼ cup unsweetened cocoa
⅛ teaspoon salt
½ cup milk

½ teaspoon vanilla
2 eggs, separated
⅓ cup plus 2 tablespoons sugar
1 cup heavy cream

Butter the bottom and sides of 2 small soufflé dishes. Make a foil collar for the outside of the dish. Make the collar so that it stands 1½-inches above the rim and butter it.

Melt butter in a saucepan over low heat. Whisk in flour. Remove from heat and add cocoa and salt. Blend in milk gradually. Return to heat and whisk until mixture boils and becomes thick. Remove from heat, add vanilla, and stir. Press plastic wrap onto surface of mixture. Set aside to cool. Beat egg yolks. Add ⅓ cup sugar gradually and beat until thick. Blend cooled chocolate mixture into the yolks.

Preheat oven to 300 degrees.

Beat egg whites in a clean, dry bowl until frothy. Add 1 tablespoon sugar gradually and beat until stiff peaks form. Add a little of the whites to the chocolate mixture to lighten it. Fold remaining whites into chocolate gently, until just blended. Pour into prepared soufflé dishes. Place dishes in a large pan containing 1-inch of water. Bake for 1 hour to 1 hour 5 minutes. Whip the cream with 1 tablespoon sugar. Serve the soufflé immediately with a large dollop of the sweetened whipped cream dropped into the broken center of the soufflé.

Preparation Time: 20 minutes
Cooking Time: 1 hour to 1 hour 5 minutes
Serves: 2

Baked Pear Custard

10 ripe but firm pears, peeled, cored,
and sliced
2 tablespoons fresh lemon juice
1⅓ cups milk
⅔ cup heavy cream
1 cup sugar

⅔ cup flour
4 large eggs
1½ teaspoons vanilla
2 tablespoons unsalted butter,
softened

Preheat oven to 425 degrees. Butter a 2½-quart baking dish.

Toss pears with lemon juice. Arrange pears decoratively on the bottom of the prepared baking dish. Blend milk, cream, ⅔ cup sugar, flour, eggs, and vanilla until mixture is just combined. Pour over pears. Sprinkle with remaining ⅓ cup sugar and dot with butter.

Bake in upper third of oven for 50 minutes or until golden and custard is set. Serve warm.

Preparation Time: 25 minutes
Cooking Time: 50
Serves: 8 to 10

Ginger Raisin Cake

1 cup butter, softened
1 cup dark brown sugar
1 cup light molasses
3 eggs
3 cups flour
1 teaspoon baking powder
1 teaspoon baking soda

1½ teaspoons cinnamon
1½ teaspoons ground cloves
1 tablespoon ground ginger
1 cup boiling water
½ cup chopped crystallized ginger
⅓ cup golden raisins

Preheat oven to 350 degrees. Oil and flour a 9 × 13-inch baking dish.

Cream butter and sugar. Add molasses and eggs, 1 at a time. Sift flour, baking powder, baking soda, cinnamon, cloves, and ginger together in a separate bowl. Stir the dry ingredients into the butter mixture, alternating with the boiling water, until well blended. Add chopped ginger and raisins. Pour into the prepared pan. Shake to level. Bake for 30 to 40 minutes or until a tester inserted in the center comes out clean.

Preparation Time: 25 minutes
Cooking Time: 30 to 40 minutes
Serves: 12

Black Bottom Cupcakes

1 cup sugar

¼ cup cocoa

1½ cups flour

½ teaspoon salt

1 teaspoon baking soda

1 cup water

⅓ cup oil

1 tablespoon vinegar

1 teaspoon vanilla

8 ounces cream cheese

⅓ cup sugar

1 egg

6 ounces semi-sweet chocolate chips

Preheat oven to 350 degrees. Line muffin cups with paper baking cups.

Sift sugar, cocoa, flour, salt, and baking soda together. Add water, oil, vinegar, and vanilla. Blend well. Set aside. Beat cream cheese, sugar, and egg. Stir in chocolate chips. Set aside.

Fill prepared muffin cups ⅓ full with the chocolate batter and top with 1 heaping tablespoon of the cream cheese mixture. Bake for 25 minutes. Cool on wire rack before serving.

Preparation Time: 20 minutes

Cooking Time: 25 minutes

Makes: 2 dozen

Note: This unique chocolate cupcake has a rich and creamy center.

Bittersweet Tweed Cake

Cake flour is a delicate, light flour, milled from soft wheat. It is the baker's choice to produce a light and feathery high-rising cake.

Cake
½ cup butter
½ cup sugar
2 cups cake flour
3 teaspoons baking powder
Salt
1 cup milk

1 teaspoon vanilla
3 squares unsweetened baking chocolate
2 egg whites
½ cup sugar

Preheat oven to 350 degrees.

Butter and flour 2 8-inch round cake pans. Cream butter and sugar. Sift dry ingredients in another bowl. Add to the creamed mixture. Add milk and vanilla. Grate chocolate and blend into the batter so that it looks like tweed (do not over-blend). Beat egg whites in a clean, dry bowl until frothy. Add 1 tablespoon sugar at a time. Beat until stiff peaks form. Fold whites into tweed batter. Pour into prepared pans. Bake for 20 to 25 minutes. Allow to cool.

Frosting
¾ cup butter, softened
3 egg yolks

2¼ cups powdered sugar

Cream butter, egg yolks, and powdered sugar together. Frost tops of both cooled cake layers and stack. Frost sides.

Topping
½ cup semi-sweet chocolate chips
2 tablespoons water

Melt chocolate chips. Add water and blend. Pour over the frosted cake allowing it to drip freely down the sides.

Preparation Time: 1 hour
Cooking Time: 20 to 25 minutes
Serves: 8 to 10

Praline Cheesecake

Crust

1 cup graham cracker crumbs
2 tablespoons sugar

3 tablespoons butter, melted

Preheat oven to 350 degrees.

Combine graham cracker crumbs, sugar, and butter. Press into the bottom and up the sides of a 9-inch springform pan. Bake for 10 minutes. Set aside to cool.

Filling

24 ounces cream cheese, softened
1 cup brown sugar, packed
4 eggs

2 cups sour cream
1½ teaspoons vanilla
¾ cup pecans, finely chopped

Beat cream cheese and brown sugar until light and creamy. Add eggs, 1 at a time, beating well after each addition. Blend in sour cream, vanilla, and nuts. Pour into crust. Bake for 1 hour 10 minutes (when done, the center will appear soft and shiny). Cool in pan on a rack.

Topping

3 ounces cream cheese, softened
⅓ cup brown sugar, packed

1 cup heavy cream, whipped

Blend cream cheese and brown sugar until smooth and creamy. Fold in whipped cream. Spread over top of cooled cheesecake. Chill for 4 hours before serving.

Preparation Time: 1 hour
Cooking Time: 1 hour 10 minutes
Serves: 8 to 10

Note: Best when prepared a day prior to serving. To prevent cheesecake from cracking, be sure not to use a pan that is too small or an oven that is too hot. Leaving the cheesecake in the oven to cool gradually will also keep it from cracking.

Black Bottom Cheesecake with Raspberry Purée

Crust

1½ cups chocolate wafer cookie crumbs

½ cup butter, melted

3 tablespoons sugar

Combine cookie crumbs, butter, and sugar. Press into the bottom and ¾ of the way up the sides of a 9-inch springform pan.

Filling

24 ounces cream cheese, softened

1 cup sugar

3 eggs

½ cup butter, softened

½ teaspoon orange extract

Preheat oven to 450 degrees.

Combine cream cheese and sugar and beat until fluffy. Add eggs, 1 at a time, beating well after each addition. Blend in butter and orange extract. Pour filling into crust and bake for 15 minutes. Lower heat to 350 degrees and continue baking for 20 minutes. Place a baking sheet on oven shelf below pan to catch drippings. Allow to cool before cutting.

Purée

1½ cups raspberries

1 teaspoon sugar

1 teaspoon lemon juice

2 tablespoons Grand Marnier

Purée raspberries. Add sugar, lemon juice, and Grand Marnier.

Pour sauce over each individual serving.

Preparation Time: 1 hour

Cooking Time: 35 minutes

Serves: 12 to 16

Cookies and Cream Cheesecake

Crust

**25 cream-filled chocolate cookies,
  crushed**

¼ cup butter, softened

Blend the crushed cookies and butter in a mixer or food processor. Press into the bottom and up the sides of a 9-inch springform pan. Set aside.

Filling

1½ cups sugar

32 ounces cream cheese, softened

4 whole eggs

3 egg yolks

2 teaspoons vanilla

2 tablespoons flour

⅓ cup heavy cream

**16 cream-filled chocolate cookies,
  chopped**

Preheat oven to 475 degrees.

Beat sugar and cream cheese together for 3 minutes. Add 4 whole eggs and 3 egg yolks, 1 at a time, beating lightly after each addition. Add vanilla, flour, and cream. Beat until light and fluffy (do not overbeat). Pour into crust alternating layers of cream mixture and chopped cookies, starting and ending with the cream mixture. Bake for 15 minutes, then reduce oven to 325 degrees and bake for 50 minutes longer. Remove from oven.

Topping

2 cups sour cream

¼ cup chocolate chips

Top with sour cream and sprinkle with chocolate chips. Bake for 10 minutes. Chill for at least 4 hours before removing from pan. Keep refrigerated.

Preparation Time: 50 minutes

Cooking Time: 1 hour 15 minutes

Serves: 8 to 10

Note: Best if prepared a day prior to serving.

Petite Sesame Shortbread

1 cup butter
½ cup sugar
2 cups flour

4 tablespoons water
Sesame seeds

Preheat oven to 325 degrees.

Cream butter and sugar. Add flour and blend. Add up to 4 tablespoons water, 1 at a time, blending until mixture resembles coarse meal. Roll into petite log shapes. Coat with sesame seeds and bake on a buttered cooking sheet for 10 to 15 minutes.

Preparation Time: 5 minutes

Cooking Time: 10 to 15 minutes

Makes: 2 dozen

Note: A wonderful cookie for children to make.

Oatmeal Lace Cookies

1 cup flour
½ teaspoon baking powder
1 cup sugar
1 cup rolled oats

4 tablespoons heavy cream
⅔ cup butter, melted
4 tablespoons light corn syrup

Preheat oven to 375 degrees.

Sift flour, baking powder, and sugar into a large bowl. Add oats, cream, butter, and corn syrup, stirring well after each addition. Drop by rounded teaspoons on a baking sheet lined with foil or parchment (do not butter). Bake for 6 to 8 minutes (do not overbake). Allow to cool completely, then remove cookies from foil or parchment.

Preparation Time: 15 minutes

Cooking Time: 6 to 8 minutes

Makes: 2 dozen

Peanut Butter Cookies with a Chocolate Bite

1½ **cups flour**
½ **cup sugar**
½ **teaspoon baking soda**
¼ **teaspoon salt**
½ **cup shortening**
½ **cup plus 6 tablespoons peanut butter**

¼ **cup corn syrup**
1 **tablespoon milk**
Oil
6 **ounces semi-sweet chocolate chips**

Combine flour, sugar, baking soda, salt, shortening, ½ cup peanut butter, corn syrup, and milk. Mix together until it resembles coarse meal. Add drops of oil if needed for mixture to stick together. Form into a long roll about 2-inches in diameter. Wrap in wax paper and chill dough until firm.

Preheat oven to 350 degrees.

Cut dough into ¼-inch thick slices. Place half of the slices on an ungreased baking sheet. Dab center of each cookie with ½ teaspoon peanut butter. Add 3 or 4 chocolate chips to the peanut butter center. Top with another slice of dough and seal by pressing the edges together with the prongs of a fork. Bake for 10 to 12 minutes.

Preparation Time: 30 minutes
Cooking Time: 10 to 12 minutes
Makes: 2 dozen

Chocolate Chip Meringue Kisses

4 egg whites

¼ teaspoon salt

1 teaspoon vanilla

1½ cups sugar

12 ounces semi-sweet chocolate chips

Preheat oven to 325 degrees. Line baking sheet with a brown paper bag.

Beat egg whites, salt, and vanilla until soft peaks form. Add sugar gradually and beat until very stiff peaks form. Fold in chocolate chips. Drop by rounded teaspoons to form kisses (kisses should be the size of a nickel or quarter). Bake for 20 to 25 minutes (do not overbake). Remove kisses before they become golden brown. Cool 1 kiss to test for doneness (kisses should be completely dry inside not soft).

Preparation Time: 15 minutes

Cooking Time: 20 to 25 minutes

Makes: 3 to 4 dozen

Note: The size of kisses and humidity will determine the cooking time. The brown bag will not burn and is great for easy removal of kisses and easy clean up.

Chocolate Dipped Macaroons

5 egg whites
2 cups ground almonds
2 cups powdered sugar, sifted
7 ounces shredded coconut
Grated peel of ½ lemon

1½ tablespoons rum
5 ounces Belgian semi-sweet baking chocolate (or any semi-sweet baking chocolate)

Preheat oven to 300 degrees. Line baking sheet with parchment.

Beat egg whites until stiff. Fold in almonds and 1 cup powdered sugar. Add coconut, remaining 1 cup powdered sugar, lemon peel, and rum. Work into a sticky dough. Drop on parchment by rounded teaspoons. Bake for 40 minutes (should be crisp and lightly golden). Cool on wire rack. Melt chocolate over low heat. Dip cooled macaroons in melted chocolate to coat a third of each. Place on wax paper to set.

Preparation Time: 30 minutes
Cooking Time: 40 minutes
Makes: 2 dozen

Chocolate Peanut Butter Squares

½ cup butter, melted
1¾ cups graham cracker crumbs
1 cup peanut butter

2⅓ cups powdered sugar
2 cups semi-sweet chocolate chips

Combine butter, graham cracker crumbs, peanut butter, and sugar. Pat into a lightly oiled 9×13-inch baking dish. Melt chocolate chips over medium heat. Pour over peanut butter mixture. Chill slightly, score the top in desired piece sizes, and chill completely. Cut along scores to serve.

Preparation Time: 20 minutes
Serves: 20

Note: May be served with a scoop of vanilla ice cream on top.

Polka Dot Brownies with White Chocolate

1 cup unsalted butter

16 ounces semi-sweet chocolate chips

4 eggs, room temperature

½ teaspoon salt

1⅓ cups sugar

2 teaspoons vanilla

½ cup flour

2 4-ounce white chocolate candy bars, broken into bits

2 cups chopped pecans

Preheat oven to 375 degrees. Lightly butter a 9 × 13-inch baking dish.

Melt butter and chocolate chips in a heavy saucepan over low heat. Remove from heat and continue stirring until smooth and satiny. Set aside. Cool to room temperature. Beat eggs until thick and light in color. Add salt and gradually add sugar while beating, about 8 minutes or until eggs reach consistency of soft peak whipped cream. Beat in vanilla. Fold cooled chocolate gently into egg mixture. Fold in flour, white chocolate, and nuts, being careful not to overwork the batter. Pour batter into the prepared baking dish. Bake for 35 minutes or until a tester inserted in the center comes out clean. Cool completely before cutting, approximately 5 hours. Store at room temperature. Do not refrigerate.

Preparation Time: 40 minutes

Cooking Time: 35 minutes

Makes: 2 dozen

Burgundy Spiced Pears

8 pears
4 cups Burgundy wine
2 cups sugar

1 stick cinnamon
2 cups heavy cream, whipped to serve

Preheat oven to 275 degrees.

Peel pears and core from the bottom, leaving stems intact. Heat wine, sugar, and cinnamon in a large saucepan. Add pears, standing them upright, and simmer for 10 minutes. Place upright pears in a baking dish. Pour wine sauce over pears. Cover and bake for 1 hour. Baste pears once during baking. Serve individually with whipped cream piped decoratively around each pear.

Preparation Time: 30 minutes
Cooking Time: 1 hour
Serves: 8

Raspberry Peach Cobbler

1 cup fresh raspberries
2 fresh peaches, peeled and sliced
2 cups flour
2 cups sugar

2 teaspoons baking powder
2 eggs
2 tablespoons butter, melted

Preheat oven to 350 degrees.

Place raspberries in a 9 × 13-inch baking dish. Top with peaches. Combine flour, sugar, and baking powder. Add eggs and blend (mixture will be dry). Pour mixture over fruit. Drizzle melted butter over top. Bake for 1 hour.

Preparation Time: 20 minutes
Cooking Time: 1 hour
Serves: 8

Note: This is a light buttery dessert that is best served in a bowl topped with heavy cream, ice cream, or whipped cream.

Frosted Oranges

6 navel oranges

1 quart vanilla ice cream, softened

6 teaspoons Amaretto or Curacao

4 egg whites

½ cup sugar

Flatten the bottom of each orange so that each stands on its own. Cut the top off each orange, measuring 1-inch down. Remove the fruit from the oranges and discard. Spoon ice cream into each orange shell and make a hole in the middle of each. Pour in 1 teaspoon of liqueur. Freeze for 4 hours.

Preheat oven to 450 degrees.

Beat egg whites, gradually adding sugar 1 teaspoon at a time until peaks form. Spread meringue generously over ice cream, sealing to the edges of the orange shells. Bake for 2 to 3 minutes or until meringue is slightly golden.

Preparation Time: 20 minutes

Cooking Time: 2 to 3 minutes

Serves: 6

Note: A California version of Baked Alaska.

Raspberry Sorbet

1 cup superfine sugar

2 cups water

4 cups fresh raspberries

4 tablespoons fresh lemon juice

Fresh raspberries for garnish

Fresh mint sprigs for garnish

Combine sugar and water in a saucepan. Bring to a boil and stir until sugar is dissolved. Allow syrup to cool. Purée raspberries. Strain raspberries through a fine sieve, pressing on the solids. Stir in syrup and lemon juice. Quick chill by setting the bowl with mixture in a larger bowl filled with ice water for 15 to 20 minutes. Stir occasionally. Freeze berry mixture in an ice cream maker according to manufacturer's instructions. Serve garnished with fresh raspberries and mint sprigs.

Preparation Time: 30 minutes

Cooking Time: 5 minutes

Makes: 2 pints

Cranberry Ice

1 package fresh cranberries
6 cups water

1 cup sugar
Fresh mint sprigs for garnish

Wash and sort through the cranberries, removing stems and any soft berries. Fill a heavy saucepan with 5 cups water. Bring to a boil and add cranberries. Boil until they reach the "popping" stage. Strain the berries through a colander, reserving the water. Crush the berries in the colander over the reserved water, using a wooden spoon to remove all of the berry juice. Place a small amount of the pressed pulp into the cranberry juice. Discard the remaining pulp. Return juice to stove. Add 1 cup water and sugar. Bring to a boil, stirring constantly. Pour into ice cube trays (approximately 3 trays) and freeze for at least 6 hours or overnight. Frappé 3 to 5 berry cubes per person just prior to serving. Garnish with fresh mint sprigs.

Preparation Time: 10 minutes

Cooking Time: Approximately 10 to 15 minutes

Makes: 42 cubes

Note: Berry cubes will keep indefinitely in plastic bags. Serve between courses or as an accompaniment to a holiday dinner.

Rum Currant Ice Cream with Walnuts

2 cups black or red currants
1½ cups dark rum
16 egg yolks
1 cup sugar

4 cups heavy cream
4 cups milk
1½ cups coarsely chopped walnuts

Soak currants in rum for 15 minutes. Scald the currants and rum in a heavy saucepan. Remove from heat and cool thoroughly. Strain currants into a separate bowl, reserving 1 cup of the liquid (add a little rum, if necessary, to measure 1 cup). Set aside. Beat egg yolks and sugar until the sugar is dissolved and the mixture is thick and pale in color. Set aside. Scald the cream and milk in a heavy saucepan. Pour 2 cups of the hot cream into the egg mixture, whisking continuously (take caution not to scramble the eggs). Pour this cream and egg mixture slowly back into the cream and milk mixture while continuing to whisk. Cook over low heat stirring constantly with a wooden spoon, until the mixture thickens enough to coat the back of the spoon. Strain through a fine sieve into a bowl and whisk a few times to cool slightly. Stir in the reserved 1 cup of liquid and chill. Freeze custard in an ice cream maker according to the manufacturer's instructions. Add the scalded currants and nuts to the ice cream during the last minutes of freezing.

Preparation Time: 40 minutes
Cooking Time: 30 minutes
Makes: 3 to 4 quarts

Pistachio Brittle Ice Cream

2 cups pistachio nuts, shelled, lightly toasted, and finely ground in a food processor
4 cups milk
4 cups cream

14 egg yolks
1⅓ cups sugar
2 teaspoons vanilla
2 cups Pistachio Brittle, coarsely ground (recipe below)

Whisk nuts, milk, and cream in a heavy saucepan. Bring to a boil over low heat. Remove from heat. Allow mixture to stand for 30 minutes, then strain through a fine sieve, pressing hard on the solids. Whisk egg yolks and sugar. Add cream mixture gradually, whisking constantly. Transfer mixture to a clean heavy saucepan and cook over very low heat, stirring constantly until the mixture thickens slightly and coats the back of a spoon. Strain mixture through a fine sieve (to eliminate lumps) into a metal bowl set in a larger bowl of ice water.

Stir in the vanilla and Pistachio Brittle gently, until blended. Cool custard, stirring occasionally. Freeze custard in an ice cream maker according to manufacturer's instructions.

Chill for 4 to 5 hours before serving.

Preparation Time: 30 minutes
Cooking Time: 1 hour
Makes: 2 quarts

Pistachio Brittle

1 cup pistachio nuts, shelled, lightly toasted, and coarsely chopped
1 tablespoon unsalted butter

¾ cup sugar
3 tablespoons water

Oil baking sheet.

Sauté pistachio nuts in butter over medium heat for 2 to 3 minutes or until golden, stirring occasionally.

Continued on next page

Combine sugar and water in a skillet. Bring mixture to a boil, rinsing down any sugar crystals clinging to the sides with a brush dipped in cold water. Stir until the sugar is dissolved. Boil syrup, swirling the pan until syrup turns a golden caramel color. Stir in pistachios. Pour mixture immediately onto prepared sheet. Allow to cool completely. Break into pieces.

Preparation Time: 25 minutes

Cooking Time: 10 minutes

Makes: ½ pound

Note: Brittle keeps in an airtight container, chilled, indefinitely.

Chocolate Sauce

3 ounces bittersweet baking chocolate

1 ounce milk chocolate

4 tablespoons unsalted butter

½ cup sugar

¼ cup water

1 tablespoon corn syrup

¼ cup condensed milk

Water to thin if needed

Melt and blend the 2 chocolates and butter in the top of a double boiler. Remove from heat. Combine sugar, water, and corn syrup in a heavy saucepan. Boil mixture until the sugar has dissolved, stirring constantly and wiping down the sides of the pan with a wet pastry brush. Reduce the heat and simmer for 5 minutes. Remove from heat.

Add corn syrup mixture and condensed milk to chocolate mixture. Beat until smooth and light. Add a little water to thin if necessary.

Preparation Time: 15 minutes

Cooking Time: 10 minutes

Makes: 1⅓ cups

Sweet Lemon Waffles with Fruited Butters

Waffles

1½ cups flour

1 teaspoon sugar

2 teaspoons baking powder

½ teaspoon salt

¼ cup butter

1 cup milk

½ cup fresh lemon juice

3 egg yolks, beaten until smooth

3 egg whites, beaten until stiff peaks form

Lemon Butter to serve (recipe page 291)

Strawberry Butter to serve (recipe page 291)

Snowy Drift to serve (recipe page 291)

Lemon Syrup to serve (recipe page 291)

Fresh strawberries for garnish

Fresh blueberries for garnish

Preheat and oil a waffle iron.

Combine flour, sugar, baking powder, and salt. Set aside. Melt butter. Beat in milk, then lemon juice, and finally egg yolks. Blend liquid ingredients into flour mixture until just moistened. Fold egg whites into batter until just blended.

Pour enough batter onto waffle iron to cover ⅔ of grid. Close iron and bake until cooked through, approximately 5 minutes.

Serve with Lemon Butter, Strawberry Butter, and Snowy Drift. Top with Lemon Syrup and garnish with fresh strawberries and blueberries.

Preparation Time: 15 minutes

Cooking Time: 20 minutes

Serves: 6

Note: Timing is important in the baking of crisp yet tender waffles. The usual guide is to wait until the waffle stops steaming. However, 1 or 2 minutes more are often needed. If the lid resists lifting, the waffle is not quite done. Cook for another minute and lift again. For a festive patriotic dessert, omit the Lemon Syrup.

Continued on next page

Lemon Butter

¼ cup unsalted butter, softened
1 teaspoon powdered sugar

2 teaspoons lemon juice

Cream butter and sugar until light and fluffy. Beat in lemon juice until blended.

Preparation Time: 5 minutes

Makes: ¼ cup

Falernum is a West Indies syrup of almond, lime, and spices. Falernum may be found in specialty liquor stores.

Strawberry Butter with Falernum

¼ cup unsalted butter, softened
2 tablespoons strawberry preserves

1 tablespoon falernum (½ tablespoon Cointreau may be substituted)

Cream butter until light and fluffy. Blend in preserves and falernum until smooth.

Preparation Time: 5 minutes

Makes: ⅓ cup

Snowy Drift

1 egg
½ cup powdered sugar, sifted
3 tablespoons butter, melted

1 teaspoon vanilla extract
1 cup heavy cream, whipped

Beat egg in a large bowl. Add sugar slowly, beating until thickened, approximately 2 minutes. Blend in butter and vanilla. Fold in whipped cream. Chill for 1 hour or more before serving.

Preparation Time: 10 minutes

Makes: 3 cups

Note: A delectable sweetened whipped cream that can be made ahead in the morning and served late into the evening without fear of separation or deflation.

Lemon Syrup

1 teaspoon grated lemon peel
1 teaspoon grated orange peel
¼ cup fresh lemon juice

¼ cup fresh orange juice
½ cup powdered sugar, sifted

Combine all ingredients and blend well.

Preparation Time: 10 minutes

Makes: Approximately 1 cup

Note: The syrup may be kept indefinitely if stored in the refrigerator. Serve at room temperature.

Gingerbread Waffles with Lemon Syrup

1 cup flour
1½ teaspoons baking powder
½ teaspoon baking soda
1 teaspoon ground ginger
¾ teaspoon ground allspice
¾ teaspoon cinnamon
¼ teaspoon salt
1 egg, separated, room temperature
⅓ cup dark brown sugar
¾ cup buttermilk

¼ cup molasses
3 tablespoons butter, melted
Pinch cream of tartar
Lemon Butter to serve
   (recipe page 291)
Snowy Drift to serve
   (recipe page 291)
Lemon Syrup to serve
   (recipe page 291)

Preheat and oil a waffle iron.

Combine flour, baking powder, baking soda, spices, and salt. Set aside. Beat egg yolk and brown sugar in medium bowl until light and fluffy. Stir in buttermilk, molasses, and butter. Blend liquid ingredients into flour mixture, stirring until just moistened. Set aside. Beat egg white with cream of tartar in a separate bowl until soft peaks form. Fold into batter.

Pour enough batter onto waffle iron to cover ⅔ of grid. Close iron and bake until cooked through, approximately 4 minutes. See timing suggestion under Waffles on recipe page 290.

Serve with Lemon Butter and Snowy Drift and top with Lemon Syrup.

Preparation Time: 20 minutes
Cooking Time: 10 minutes
Serves: 4

Note: The tangy sweet citrus taste of the Lemon Syrup enhances the gingerbread flavor.

Preceding
pages feature:
Sweet Lemon
Waffles with
Fruited Butters;
Gingerbread
Waffles with Lemon
Syrup; Brownie
Waffles with Warm
Banana Sauce;
Black Bottom
Cheesecake with
Raspberry Purée
Sauce; Celery Seed
Dip with Fresh Fruit.

Brownie Waffles with Warm Banana Sauce

Waffles

1½ cups cake flour

¾ cup sugar

½ cup unsweetened cocoa powder

1 teaspoon baking powder

½ teaspoon baking soda

¼ teaspoon salt

¼ teaspoon nutmeg

½ cup butter

1½ cups buttermilk

2 eggs

1 teaspoon vanilla extract

½ cup finely chopped pecans

Warm Banana Sauce to serve
   (recipe below)

Snowy Drift to serve
   (recipe page 291)

Chocolate syrup to serve

Preheat and oil waffle iron.

Sift together flour, sugar, cocoa, baking powder, baking soda, salt, and nutmeg. Set aside. Melt butter. Beat in buttermilk, then eggs and vanilla. Stir liquid ingredients into dry mixture until just blended. Fold in nuts. Pour enough batter onto waffle iron to cover ⅔ of grid. Close iron and bake until cooked through, approximately 5 minutes. Serve with Warm Banana Sauce. Top with Snowy Drift and chocolate syrup.

Preparation Time: 15 minutes

Cooking Time: 20 minutes

Serves: 6

Note: Sure to evoke sighs of satisfaction, this rich, fudge-like dessert has a wonderful aroma and flavor. Any flavor ice cream is a tasty accompaniment. See timing suggestion under Waffles on recipe page 290.

Warm Banana Sauce

4 bananas, well ripened

1 cup heavy cream

⅓ cup sugar

2½ tablespoons dark rum

1 teaspoon vanilla extract

Preheat oven to 350 degrees.

Roast bananas in their skins on a baking sheet for 20 minutes. Peel bananas and mash. Stir in cream, sugar, rum, and vanilla.

Preparation Time: 10 minutes

Cooking Time: 20 minutes

Makes: 3 cups

Cranberry Nests

Nests
8 sheets phyllo
1 cup butter, melted

6 tablespoons fine dry unseasoned bread crumbs

Defrost the unopened package of phyllo thoroughly. Lay out sheets. Cover the stack of phyllo immediately and completely with plastic wrap and then a damp tea towel (do not let the damp towel touch the phyllo).

Lay out a single sheet of phyllo. Brush evenly with a thin layer of butter. Sprinkle with bread crumbs. Repeat once, then finish with a plain sheet on top. Cut with a pizza cutter or scissors into 4-inch squares. Repeat this entire procedure making 1 more phyllo, butter, and breadcrumb stack.

Preheat oven to 350 degrees.

Brush 24 medium muffin cups with butter. Fit squares, corners up, into each cup. Bake for 10 to 12 minutes or until golden. Cool for 5 minutes in pan and remove to a rack to finish cooling.

Filling
11 ounces cream cheese, room temperature

⅓ cup powdered sugar, sifted
Zest and juice of 1 lemon

Whip cream cheese, sugar, lemon zest, and juice. Set aside.

Cranberry Topping
16 ounces whole cranberry sauce
1 tablespoon Grand Marnier

½ cup sliced almonds, toasted

Blend cranberry sauce with Grand Marnier until smooth.

Spoon cream cheese filling into nests, filling a third. Spoon in 2 to 3 teaspoons of cranberry mixture and top with toasted almonds.

Preparation Time: 40 minutes
Cooking Time: 10 to 12 minutes
Makes: 24

Note: May be made 4 hours ahead and refrigerated. The unfilled nests may be made a day ahead and kept in plastic bags.

Crispy Pecan Puffs

Brown sugar owes both its color and flavor to the small amount of molasses that clings to the sugar crystals during processing.

1 cup brown sugar, packed
2 tablespoons ground pecans
1 tablespoon cornstarch
1 tablespoon bourbon or dark rum

1 egg white, room temperature
Pinch cream of tartar
Salt
2 cups pecan halves

Preheat oven to 300 degrees.

Sift brown sugar. Add ground pecans and cornstarch. Add bourbon and blend well. Set aside. Beat the egg white with cream of tartar and salt until it holds stiff peaks. Stir a third of the egg white into the sugar mixture and blend well. Add remaining white to the sugar mixture (it will become more liquid). Add pecan halves, stirring gently to coat well. Arrange pecans individually, rounded side up, in a small mound of batter 2-inches apart on a buttered baking sheet. Bake for 12 minutes or until puffed and golden brown. Allow puffs to cool on the sheet for 1 minute. Transfer to a wire rack and allow to cool completely. Keep puffs in an airtight container.

Preparation Time: 10 minutes
Cooking Time: 12 minutes
Makes: 80 to 100 puffs

Note: Puffs will keep up to 5 days.

Truffles Framboise

Truffles
8 ounces white chocolate
4 tablespoons heavy cream

2 teaspoons Chambord (raspberry liqueur)
½ cup sifted powdered sugar

Place the white chocolate in a food processor. Process into a fine grind (do not remove from processor). Boil cream and add liqueur. Pour cream mixture through feed tube of processor with motor running. Process until smooth, scraping sides and bottom. Pour truffle mixture into a bowl and place in freezer for about 30 minutes to set.

Spoon individual bite size truffle mounds on a wax paper lined baking sheet that has been dusted with powdered sugar. Return truffles to freezer until firm yet pliable.

Roll the chilled mounds into balls, dusting hands and truffles with powdered sugar.

Shells
16 ounces white chocolate

Fresh raspberries or candied violets for garnish

Special Equipment
Warming plate
Wax paper

Thin rubber gloves
Paper candy cups

Melt the white chocolate over low heat. Remove from heat. Place pan with melted chocolate on a warming plate set to *lowest* temperature setting. Place a wax paper lined baking sheet immediately next to the pan.

Remove truffles from the freezer 1 at a time for dipping. Use 2 fingers to cradle the frozen centers. Dip truffles into warm chocolate to coat entirely. Stir chocolate between dippings to maintain an even temperature. Shake off excess chocolate and place on wax paper.

Continued on next page

Garnish tops of each truffle with a fresh raspberry or candied violet. Refrigerate to set completely.

Peel the firm truffles from the wax paper while wearing the rubber gloves and place in candy cups.

Preparation Time: 2 hours

Makes: 20

Note: Truffles will keep refrigerated for about 10 days.

Crunchy Pecan Caramel Corn

24 cups popped corn, unpopped kernels removed
2 cups pecan halves
2½ cups brown sugar

¾ cup white corn syrup
1¼ cups butter
1 teaspoon baking soda

Preheat oven to 250 degrees. Oil 2 large baking sheets lightly.

Place popped corn into a very large bowl. Sprinkle pecans over top of the popcorn. Set aside. Combine brown sugar, corn syrup, and butter into a large saucepan and heat over a low flame, stirring occasionally. Bring mixture to a boil. Allow to boil for a full 5 minutes. Add baking soda and stir (mixture will foam and volume will double). Pour sugar mixture immediately over popcorn. Toss popcorn gently with a wooden spoon until completely coated. Pour the caramel corn onto the prepared baking sheets and pat down evenly. Bake for 30 minutes. Rotate pans and bake for another 30 minutes. Allow to cool. Break into pieces and store in airtight containers.

Preparation Time: 20 minutes
Cooking Time: 1 hour
Makes: 26 cups

Note: Makes a great holiday treat.

Beverages

Beer Margaritas

Photograph appears with Table of Contents.

6 ounces frozen limeade concentrate

6 ounces beer (regular or light)

6 ounces tequila

Ice

Lime wedges for garnish

Place limeade, beer, and tequila in a blender and fill container with ice. Blend until slushy. Garnish rim of glass with a wedge of lime and serve.

Preparation Time: 10 minutes

Serves: 3 to 4

Senrikas

1 small can pink lemonade
concentrate (use same can for
measuring remaining ingredients)

1 can light cream

1 can vodka or gin

Ice

Combine liquid ingredients in a blender, using the small empty can of pink lemonade as a measuring cup. Add ice to desired consistency. Blend until smooth.

Preparation Time: 5 minutes

Serves: 4

Note: The cool pink of this brunch drink disguises the delicious tangy lemon bite.

Bermuda Rum Swizzles

Oregate syrup is a heavy, thick corn syrup with a slight almond flavor used primarily as a sweetener for beverages.

9 ounces dark rum

7½ ounces pineapple juice

7½ ounces falernum or oregate syrup

5½ ounces Rose's lime juice

1¼ ounces Cointreau

Ice

Combine all ingredients except ice in a large bowl. Pour over ice to serve.

Preparation Time: 10 minutes

Serves: 8

Peach Mesa

1 cup orange juice

6 ice cubes

2 ounces peach schnapps

2 scoops vanilla ice cream

1 fresh peach, sliced and tossed with lemon juice

Blend orange juice, ice cubes, and peach schnapps in a blender until ice cubes are crushed. Add the ice cream and blend again for 30 seconds or until frothy. Pour into glasses and garnish with fresh peach slices.

Preparation Time: 8 minutes

Serves: 4

Strawberry Zinger Punch

32 ounces frozen strawberries
½ cup sugar
⅔ cup port
4 lime slices

3 fresh mint sprigs
Salt
3 quarts white wine

Combine all ingredients except white wine and bring to a boil. Reduce heat and simmer for 10 to 15 minutes. Cool, strain, and chill. Blend in wine. Serve hot or cold.

Preparation Time: 20 minutes
Makes: Approximately 3½ quarts

Sun Kissed Punch

3 eggs, separated
2 cups milk
⅓ cup sugar

1 cup heavy cream
1 teaspoon vanilla
4⅔ cups orange juice

Beat egg yolks until thick and light in color. Stir in milk. Set aside. Beat egg whites until soft peaks form. Beat sugar into egg whites, a little at a time, until stiff peaks form. Set aside. Whip the cream and vanilla. Fold the egg yolk mixture into the beaten egg whites. Fold in the whipped cream. Place mixture in a punch bowl. Fold in orange juice. Chill for 1 hour before serving.

Preparation Time: 20 minutes
Serves: 12

Frothy Pineapple Fizz

1 lime	2 tablespoons lime juice
Sugar	1 egg white
¾ cup pineapple juice	½ cup crushed ice
2 ounces gin	

Cut 2 slices from the center of the lime for garnish. Cut a slit halfway through each slice. Cut a wedge from remaining lime and moisten rim of glasses. Dip rims into sugar. Set glasses and garnish aside.

Combine pineapple juice, gin, lime juice, and egg white with crushed ice in a blender. Blend until smooth and frothy. Pour drinks into prepared glasses and garnish with lime slices.

Preparation Time: 15 minutes

Serves: 2

Minted Ice Tea

1 cup sugar
2 quarts plus 1 cup boiling water
3 lemons, juiced
4 mint sprigs

4 tea bags, English breakfast
  preferred
Ice

Combine sugar, 1 cup boiling water, lemon juice, and mint sprigs in a large pitcher. Stir well. Pour 2 quarts boiling water over tea bags in another pitcher. Allow to stand for 20 minutes. Pour tea into sugar mixture, making sure sugar is dissolved. Pour over ice.

Preparation Time: 10 minutes
Makes: 2 quarts

Note: This recipe may also be made with 1 cup orange juice and 2 cups ginger-ale, added when cooled. For a variation with spirits, add 1 ounce vodka or gin to each 6-ounce glass.

Mexican Coffee

1 ounce Kahlua
½ ounce brandy
Dash cinnamon
1 teaspoon chocolate syrup

1 cup hot coffee
Heavy cream, whipped
1 stick cinnamon or ground cinnamon
  for garnish

Place Kahlua, brandy, dash cinnamon, and chocolate syrup in a large coffee cup. Fill with hot coffee. Stir to blend. Top with whipped cream. Garnish with cinnamon stick or dust with ground cinnamon.

Preparation Time: 5 minutes
Serves: 1

Yuletide Coffee

1 teaspoon clover honey
2 tablespoons white Crème de Menthe
1 cup hot coffee

Heavy cream, whipped
Cocoa for garnish

Combine honey and Crème de Menthe in a 6-ounce cup. Fill with coffee and top with whipped cream. Dust with cocoa.

Preparation Time: 5 minutes

Serves: 1

Note: Chocolate or chocolate almond flavored coffee may be used for variation.

Frozen Holiday Egg Nog

12 eggs, separated
½ to ¾ cup powdered sugar
1 quart rum or bourbon

3 quarts natural vanilla ice cream, softened
Freshly grated nutmeg for garnish

Beat egg yolks with sugar until light yellow. Add rum or bourbon. Beat egg whites until very stiff and fold into egg yolk mixture. Add ice cream, a little at a time, beating until smooth. Store in freezer at least 1 week prior to serving to allow flavors to mellow. Serve with a dash of nutmeg.

Preparation Time: 30 minutes

Serves: 40 4-ounce cups

Note: May be stored up to 4 weeks in freezer. If mixture becomes too hard, blend in mixer.

Citrus Punch

¼ cup sugar
8 cups water
9 whole cloves
2 sticks cinnamon

4 cups apple cider
2 cups orange juice
2 cups pineapple juice
4 tablespoons lemon juice

Boil sugar in water for 10 minutes. Add cloves and cinnamon and allow to stand for 1 hour. Strain liquid. Add cider, orange juice, pineapple juice, and lemon juice. Bring to a boil. Serve warm.

Preparation Time: 15 minutes

Cooking Time: 1 hour 30 minutes

Serves: 25

Note: This punch is a great thirst quencher served over ice in warm weather.

Golden Maria

1 ounce Tia Maria
1 ounce Grand Marnier

1 ounce Cuervo Gold tequila

Combine ingredients in a brandy snifter. Warm by igniting.

Preparation Time: 5 minutes

Serves: 1

Raspberry Wave

The Raspberry Wave
and The Final Wave
are compliments of
The Wave
Restaurant, known
for its spirited
beverages.

2 ounces light rum
1 ounce Amaretto
½ ounce Cointreau
**2 teaspoons passion fruit juice
  (optional)**

20 fresh raspberries
4 ounces sweet and sour mix
Fresh raspberries for garnish
Fresh mint sprigs for garnish
Ice

Shake liquors and passion fruit juice together. Pour over ice, dividing between 2 old fashioned glasses. Blend raspberries with sweet and sour mix until frothy. Spoon on top of poured drinks, dividing evenly between the glasses. Stir once or twice to just slightly blend. Garnish with skewers of raspberries, topping with fresh mint sprigs.

Preparation Time: 15 minutes

Serves: 2

Note: This frothy, raspberry red cooler provides the perfect opener for your summertime get-togethers. Passion fruit juice is available in health food and gourmet grocery stores.

The Final Wave

½ ounce vodka
½ ounce Southern Comfort
½ ounce Midori (melon liqueur)
½ ounce Blue curacao

1 ounce pineapple juice
½ ounce sweet and sour mix
Splash of orange juice

Combine ingredients and shake or stir. Pour into a chilled glass.

Preparation Time: 5 minutes

Serves: 1

Acknowledgements

Flower Donations

Flower Fashions, *Beverly Hills*

Milo Bixby, Inc., *Los Angeles and San Marino*

Chris Slack, Flower Artist, *Los Angeles*

Food Donations

Fish King, *Glendale*

Jurgensen's, *Pasadena*

Prop Donations

Freehand, *Los Angeles*
  Julie Bagish
  John Curry
  Steven Portigal

Geary's, *Beverly Hills*

Lynne Deutch Ltd., *Los Angeles*

Mary Fenimore's Antiques, *Sierra Madre*

Tesoro Collection, Inc., *Los Angeles*

The Pavilion at Tanner Market, *Pasadena*

The Prince's Table, *Beverly Hills*

White River Furniture, *Arcadia*

Williams-Sonoma, *Beverly Hills*

A special thank you to
  Maryrose Passarelli Caspary
  Ann Morrissey Liebig
  Caroline Eshman Liebig
  Carol Morrissey Patterson
and to all the other
Junior League of Los Angeles
members who so graciously
donated props for photography
purposes.

Wine Recommendations

The California Eight
  David Barry
  James Econn
  Warner Henry
  Jerry Magnin
  William Martin
  Fred Roberts
  Grafton Tanguery
  Steve Wallace

Recipe Contributors

Gayellen Gard Albright

Harriet Daly Alders

Marla Robe Alders

Jill Jelenko Angen

Corwyn Anthony, The Wave Restaurant

Hillary Apelbaum

Susan Wright Armistead

Ladonna Arnold

Assunta DiCicco Asci

Gwendolyn Hatten Baker

Vicki Lucas Baker

Jeri Barchilon

Kathy Kevorkian Basmajian

Carolann Paul Bennett

Barbara Austin Bundy

Sybyle Burkhart

Linda Burum

Kathryn Akerman Cairns

Linda Carnegie

Debora Scalzo Centioli

Patricia Joan Cole-Ford

Steven Cooperman, M.D.

Dorothy Corcoran

Kathleen Costa

Suzanne Reese Coulter

Jovon Shaper Courtney

Patricia Cramer

Lucia Detrick

Pamela Shields Diddie

Maureen Shannon Diekmann

Leslie Dixon

Leslie Watson Doheny

Diane Elisabeth Elcan

Janet Risi Field

Linda Friedman

Julia Russell Gans

Jeanette Clark Gard

Susan Negrelli Genter

Gayle Ann Godwin

Barbara Gregory

Sharon Gustaves

Sally Hamilton

Betsy Hamilton

Marcia Hansen

Michelle Keating Hayden

Margaret Henderson

Rosemary Nielsen Hendler

Cathleen Collins Hession

Susan Christina Hiscock

Valerie Smith Holberton

Gary Hoover

Lucy Hiltabrand Hoover

Sharyn Brickey Hudson

Elizabeth Fore Hunsaker

Ann Upham Hutchinson

Mary Ann Irvine

Jennifer Iselen

Melinda Jansen Jacobson

Karen Sheahan Johnston

Christie Katona

Kelly Ann Kavanaugh

Paula Gaddis Keating

Jean Gaddis Keating

JoAnn King

Michelle Koerner

Marina Moretti Kunz

Cathy Lawless

Victoria Davies Leck

Gail Lee

Eve Rawlinson Lee

Cathy Ann Letizia

Ellen Arnow Lipson

Leslie Henning Lizotte

Audrey Lloyd

Douglass Williams Mabee

Prudence Mather Mabee

Linda Markman

Maria Mabee Mason

Lynn Baran McCarthy

Joan Tisdall McLaughlin

Kim Meredith

Cynthia Hendrick Meyer

Marian Miller

Carolyn Murphy Milner

Lauren Killian Mintie

Molly Moroney

Barbara Van Leeuwen Mullaney

Susan Mullen

Laura Newman

Jacqueline Nichols

Michael Norell

Anne Smith O'Connell

Stephanie Wolfe Ogden

Lorraine Oliver

Vicki Paneitz

Robin Patterson Nenninger

Arlene May Pettise

Tina Hansen Phillips

Joan Marie Ploetz

Barbara Pratt

Rebecca's Restaurant

Linda Regensburger

Marilyn Reisner

Mary Roberts Ripley

Diane Henderson Russell

Newton Requa Russell, Senator

Diane Christine Ryan

Jean Downey Saint

Jane Matthews Sample

Cynthia Nichols Sawyer

Nancy Armistead Schanzlin

Deborah May Scherer

Sherry Russell Sclafani

Ines Venti Sclafani

P. K. Sheldon, Ma Cuisine

Cheryl Seltzer Shiner

Darlene Doriot Skeels

Michelle Soghomonian

Lindsey Stewart

Carolyn Bonner Taff

Sarah Tenaglia

Alison Holland Thompson

Joan Coulter Tomlinson

Jane Spangler Tritt

Jodi Craig Vettese

Candace Watts Waldron

Robyn Alisson Watson

Ellen Kessler Weitman

Linda Mekeal Wessen

West Beach Cafe

Susan White

Sally Wilcox

Teri Wilde

Carole Knaul Williams

Tracey Lin Williamson-De Bello

Barbara Ann Wright

Index

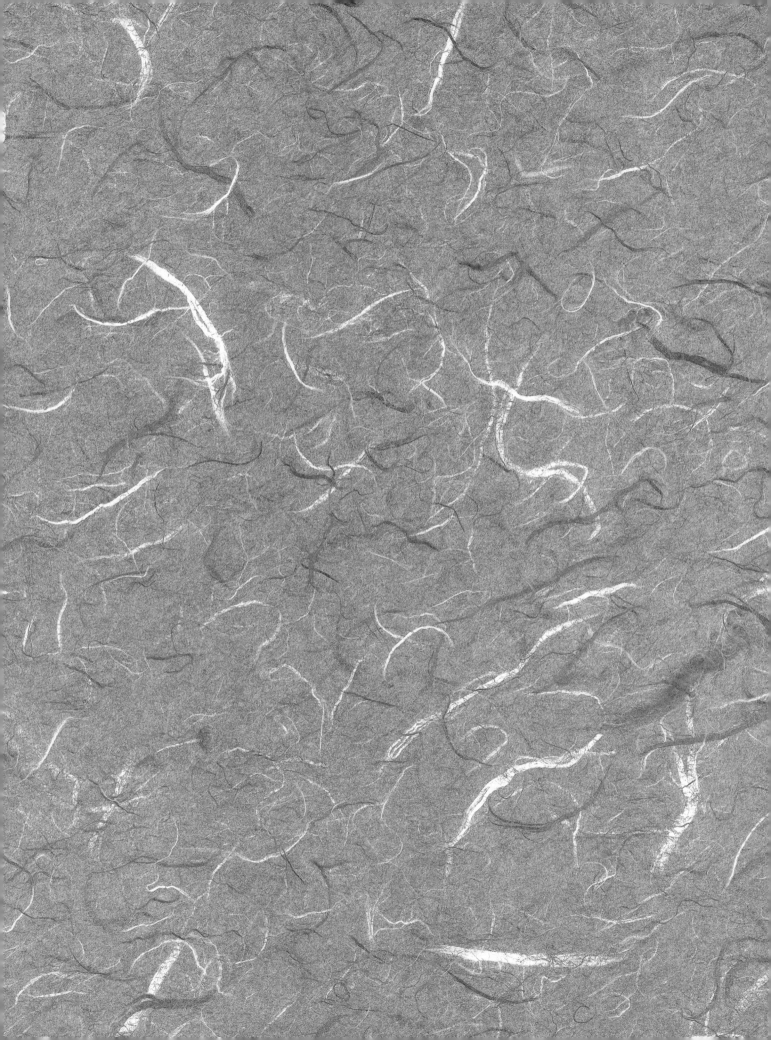